# THIS IS
# ZIMBABWE

# THIS IS
# ZIMBABWE

*Gerald Cubitt · Peter Joyce*

First published in the UK in 1992 by
New Holland (Publishers) Ltd
24 Nutford Place, London W1H 6DQ

Second edition 1996

Text © Peter Joyce 1992, 1996
Photographs © Gerald Cubitt 1992, 1996, with the exception of
the following which have been reproduced with kind permission
of the copyright owners:
Colin Bell / African Images: page 20; Mike Coppinger: pages 18,
74 bottom, 83 top, 96 top left; Ministry of Information: pages
27, 28; National Archives of Zimbabwe: page 25; Brendan
Ryan / African Images: pages 13, 15, 21 bottom, 126 bottom;
Brendan Ryan: page 107 bottom; Mark van Aardt: pages 70,
110 bottom, 111 top, 122.

Project Co-ordinator: Marje Hemp
Editorial assistants: Pippa Parker, Geoff Payne
Designer: Tamsyn Ivey
Cartographer: Angus Carr
Phototypeset by Struik DTP, Cape Town
Originated by Unifoto (Pty) Ltd, Cape Town
Printed and bound by Tien Wah Press (Pte) Ltd, Singapore

ISBN 1 85368 739 1

ACKNOWLEDGEMENTS
The photographer would like to thank the many people and
organisations who assisted him during his stay in Zimbabwe, in
particular: The Ministry of Information; The Ministry of Tourism
and Wildlife for allowing photography in the national parks; Roy
Meiring of the Cresta Hotel Group; Cresta Jameson and Cresta
Oasis hotels (Harare); Cresta Churchill Hotel (Bulawayo);
Pamuzinda Safari Lodge (Selous); Cresta Sandstone Safaris;
Mark Sparrow of Lone Star Ranch; Jeff and Victoria Stutchbury
of Chikwenya Safari Camp; Rob and Shirley Clifford, and Dave
Christianson of Fothergill Island Safaris; Tiger Bay Safari Resort;
Bill Bruce of Caribbea Bay Safari Hotel; John Burton and Andy
Williamson of Ivory Safari Lodge (Hwange); Gordon Addams of
Inn on the Vumba; Chipangali Wildlife Orphanage (Bulawayo);
National Railways of Zimbabwe (Bulawayo); Crocodile Ranch
(Victoria Falls); Smirnoff Vodka (Victoria Falls aerials), and Mary
(Fred) Forrest of Falls Craft Village.
   The Publishers would like to add their thanks to Karen
Upritchard of the Zimbabwe Tourist Development Corporation,
and Paul Tingay, text consultant for this project.

**OPPOSITE:** *Sandstone cliffs in the Gonarezhou National Park.*
**PREVIOUS PAGES:** *The magnificent Victoria Falls, Zimbabwe's
premier tourist attraction.*

# ZIMBABWEAN PROFILE

At the head of the green and pleasant Mutirikwe river-valley, just to the south-west of Masvingo, is a massive complex of high-walled granite structures. Ancient of origin and handsome to the eye, they stand silent and stark against the clear blue African sky, their more imposing elements the hilltop dzimba dzembabwe, or 'houses of stone', that once served as a grandly regal enclosure, bastion of the great 13th-century Karanga king Chigwagu Rozvingo and the heart of a settlement numbering perhaps 40 000 people; a smaller inter-leading area where powerful spirit mediums conducted their secret and portentous rituals; a nearby cave from which the mediums spoke to the people, and another enclosure where craftsmen once carved mystical soapstone emblems and fashioned jewellery from the gold and iron mined in the region.

Below in the valley lies what Europeans call The Temple, created for Mateya, wife of Chigwagu's successor. Mateya was venerated for her strong character, her love potions and for her talent for making rain. Skilled Venda builders constructed the walls of her palace from nearly a million interlocking pieces of hard granite (mortar was unknown in that time and place), decorated parts of them with chevron patterns and erected within their bounds a large cone-shaped tower resembling a giant grain basket, symbol of abundance.

These awe-inspiring edifices are the ruins of Great Zimbabwe, remains of an all-powerful but now long-gone culture that bequeathed its name, and something of its soul, to one of Africa's younger independent states.

Zimbabwe, known as Southern Rhodesia in the colonial days and as plain Rhodesia during the years of white rebellion that ended in 1980, is a large and landlocked country that sprawls

LEFT: *The splendid view from Great Zimbabwe's hill complex.*
ABOVE: *An imposing outcrop in the Matobo Hills region.*

over the sunlit grasslands of south-central Africa, its 390 000 km² bordering Zambia in the northwest, Mozambique in the north-east and east, South Africa in the south and Botswana in the southwest. It also shares a tiny stretch of frontier with the even younger republic of Namibia: its western extremity, a few kilometres from Victoria Falls, touches the eastern point of the Caprivi strip.

A rich land, economically advanced by African standards. And an extremely attractive one as well, warm in its hospitality, endowed with a magnificent wildlife heritage, blessed by a scenic variety and splendour that is seen at its best, perhaps, during the southern summer.

Between November and February almost daily rainstorms feed the hungry rivers and cleanse the countryside, bringing colour and glorious life to the plains of the central plateau, to the forested hills of the east, and to the lush plantations and mopane woodlands of the southeastern lowveld. Wintertime is less visually pleasing: this is the dry season and the terrain is duller hued, the horizons blurred by dust and the rising smoke of bush fires.

But winter has its own charms, and it is favoured by many of the half-million or so people who visit Zimbabwe each year. They choose this time because the sun is seldom too strong for comfort – winter days have a gently seductive warmth about them; the nights and early mornings are cool, often downright chilly but invigoratingly so – and because this is when the wild animals of the parks congregate around what moisture there is. They parade in their thousands in the vicinity of streams and waterholes, delighting the eye, creating images that linger in the mind long after one has departed.

# THE LAND

The Victoria Falls, the Mosi-oa-Tunya ('Smoke that Thunders') of the indigenous people and made known to the western world by the missionary and traveller David Livingstone in the mid-1850s, is one of the most spectacular of the world's natural wonders. During the peak April period the waters, flowing at 620 000 kilolitres a minute (equivalent to four times Johannesburg's yearly consumption), plunge over the 1 700-metre rim in a series of grand cataracts, throwing up a cloud of spray that, on a clear day, can be seen 70 km away and which, during the new-moon phase, produces an eerily eye-catching lunar rainbow. To get to one of the viewing points you walk through the rainforest, an entrancing place of moist, tangled undergrowth and trees whose leaves glisten and drip in the fine mist.

The falls, over twice as deep and wide as their Niagara cousins, are the best-known feature of the mighty Zambezi River that rises in the Lunda uplands far to the north, running south and then east to form the Zambia-Zimbabwe border before entering Mozambique to discharge into the Indian Ocean a full 3 540 km from its source. At the Kariba gorge, some 450 km downstream from the falls, the river has been dammed to create a 300km-

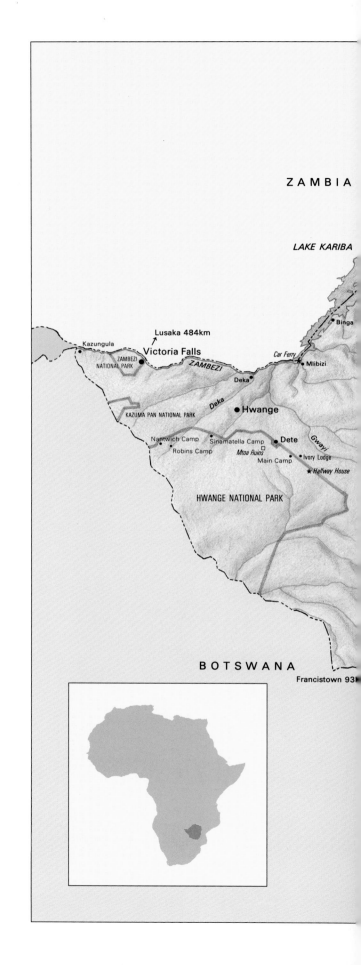

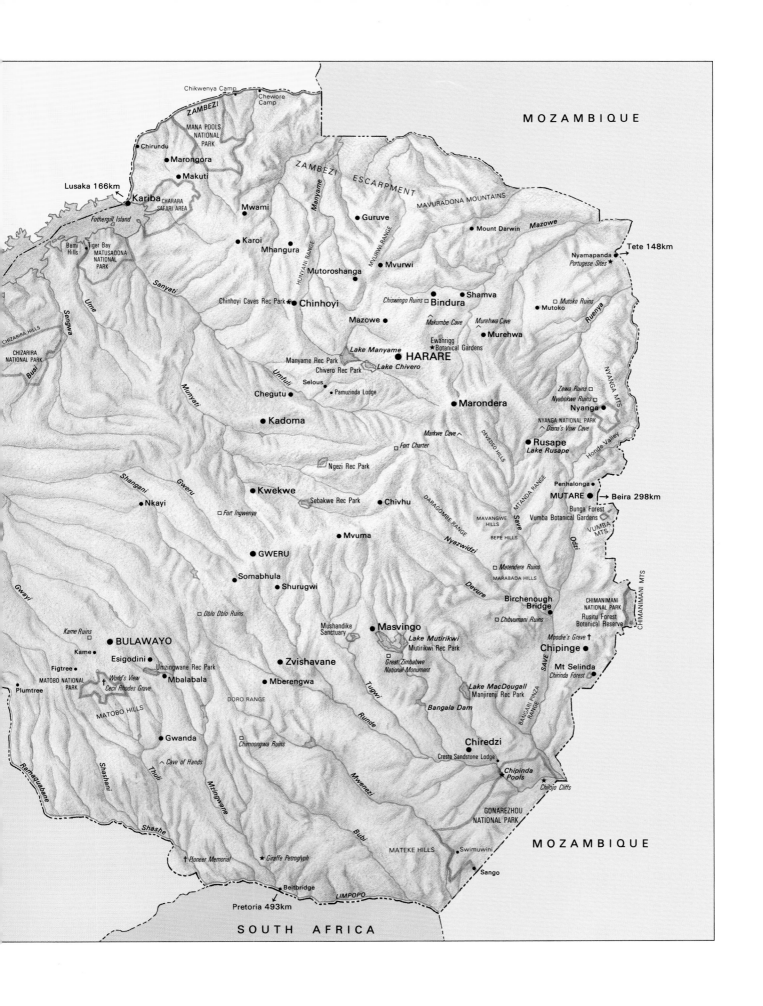

long, 5 000-km² lake that is both a holidaymaker's paradise and a generous source of protein-rich kapenta fish, about 15 000 tonnes of which are caught by commercial fishermen each year. The dam itself, of the concrete arch type and completed in 1959, is an impressive 128 metres in height, and it supplies Zimbabwe, and Zambia, with around 6 700 million kilowatt hours of cheap hydro-electric power each year.

Another river, Kipling's great and grey Limpopo, forms the country's southern boundary with South Africa.

Between the two river systems is the Highveld watershed, a broad ridge rising up to 1 500 metres above sea level and extending the length of the country, from the semi-arid southwest to the lofty Nyanga uplands in the northeast. Slicing through the Highveld is what is known as the Great Dyke, a long (515 km), narrow (up to 11 km), geologically fascinating and mineral-rich complex of immensely ancient igneous rocks aligned along a gigantic fault that is believed to be associated with the more renowned African Rift Valley system.

The Highveld covers about a quarter of the country, the terrain sloping on either side of the central ridge a further two-fifths. Below these slopes, to the southeast, is the Lowveld, a bone-dry, sunscorched and once fever-ridden plain cut through by the Save and Runde rivers. Most of the Lowveld is barely productive, its leached soils and sparse grasses supporting scattered herds of rangy cattle and communities of people who have learned to live with drought. Parts of it, though – those towards the east, around Triangle and the pretty little town of Chiredzi – have been irrigated and the now lush-looking land yields bountiful crops of sugarcane, citrus and winter wheat.

For sheer scenic enchantment, though, few regions of Zimbabwe, and indeed few places in the world, can compete with the high mountain wall that runs down the country's eastern border, from the rugged Nyanga range in the north through the more rounded, tree-mantled, misty hills of the Vumba to the stark majesty of the Chimanimani in the south. Below the hills are wide, beautiful and immensely fertile valleys: the Honde, the Burma and the Cashel, in particular, yield fine harvests of tea, coffee, fruit. Tea is also grown on the eastern slopes of the Nyanga, and some of the high country is given over to plantations of pine and wattle, but for the most part the mountains, magnificent in their vistas, lovely in their evergreen luxuriance, remain untouched by man. Indeed, some of the plantations have recently been removed, so returning the land to the mountain acacias and the wild flowers.

## CLIMATE

Zimbabwe lies within the tropics but is blessed with a temperate climate, the summer heat moderated (in most areas) by the high altitude. Winters are clear-skied and, as mentioned, cool to warm during the day and cold at night.

This is a summer-rainfall region. Great cumulonimbus clouds build up during mid- to late afternoon from about October (locals will tell you this is 'suicide month', and indeed it can be sticky, but the discomforts are exaggerated) and the rains proper begin during November. In good years, that is – too often in recent times they have been both late and meagre, and drought has withered the pastures and the maize fields.

Rainfall increases as you travel from the fringes of the Kalahari desert in the southwest to the high country of the northeast. Beitbridge, the southern border town, gets about 400 mm a year; Chipinge, in the eastern uplands, receives a generous 1 100 mm. Daytime temperatures range between 20 and 27°C in summer and a tolerable 14 and 19°C in winter.

# THE PEOPLE

Zimbabwe has a population of something over 10,5 million (1992 estimate), 95 percent of which comprises Shona and Si'Ndebele speaking Africans.

White settlement began in 1890 but never reached flood-like proportions, and when the colonial era finally ended, 90 years later, Zimbabweans of European extraction numbered a modest 200 000. However, immigrants and the descendants of immigrants remain prominent in the country's industrial, business and commercial farming sectors. Among other minority groups are people of Indian origin, the small Afro-European community, and some 300 000 guest-workers, most of whom come from neighbouring Malawi and Mozambique.

The rate of natural increase, at an estimated 35 per thousand annually – which means a doubling of the population every 20 years – is one of the world's highest, a source of serious concern to those who run a country where jobs are scarce and the potential for economic growth limited.

Three-quarters of Zimbabweans are under the age of 30, about 45 percent under 15. Population density across the land is around 25 per square kilometre, though on average of course the countryside supports rather fewer: about a quarter of the people are concentrated in and around the towns.

Rapid urbanization, indeed, is one of the more striking features of the Zimbabwean socio-economic scene – as it is in the rest of the developing world. Here, though, it received an artificial and tragic impetus during the liberation struggle of the 1970s, a low-intensity but hugely destructive war of attrition that displaced hundreds of thousands of rural families.

The majority of Zimbabweans – around 70 percent – belong to the Shona peoples of the country's central and eastern regions, of whom there are five main, culturally related groupings: the Karanga, Zesuru, Nyika, Ndau and Korekore. Smaller communities are the Tonga, who inhabit both sides of the Zambezi River in the northwest, and the Vendao and Hlengwe people of the southwest and east.

The Shona are descendants of Bantu-speaking migrants who began filtering down from the Great Lakes region of East Africa some 2 000 years ago and of their successors, more culturally advanced peoples who arrived before the 10th century AD.

Much of Shona art and craft – the once-famed ironwork, for instance, and the music – are in decline, the traditional cultural fabric weakened by increasingly close contact with and adoption of western ways. The more visible legacies of ancient custom and usage, such as costume, regalia and ornamentation, have all but disappeared. However, pottery still flourishes, and there has been a renaissance of Shona sculpture (see page 12). The abstracts, too – religious beliefs, some of the rituals, the values, the assumptions underlying relationships and so forth - have resisted the onslaught of alien cultures, especially in the more remote country areas.

OPPOSITE PAGE: *The broad reaches of the Zambezi River, seen from a point just above Victoria Falls.*
ABOVE: *This family group, dressed in its Sunday best, is on its way to church in the Eastern Highlands region.*

Shona religious conviction, which co-exists comfortably with Christianity (three quarters of indigenous Zimbabweans are Christian or part-Christian), has four major emphases: a Supreme Being (Mwari); animism, which ascribes personas, or souls, to the elements and to such natural objects as lakes, rivers, rocks and trees; the veneration of ancestors, who exert a powerful influence on the welfare of their descendants, and lastly the importance of spirit mediums, or diviners (Ngangas), who act as intermediaries between the dead and the living. The mediums are often herbalists as well, healers who, for centuries, have filled the role of doctors in the traditional communities. In that capacity their prime function is to treat sickness, not by interceding with the ancestral spirits but by collecting and dispensing herbs and other medicinal flora of the veld, many of which are known to have valuable curative properties.

The largest of Zimbabwe's minority groups is that of the Ndebele, formerly known as the Matabele, centred around the southwestern city of Bulawayo. Their forefathers were a dissident segment of the eastern Nguni (now loosely classed as Zulu) of South Africa's Natal province, whose long odyssey began when Mzilikazi, one of Shaka Zulu's ablest commanders, quarrelled with his sovereign and fled into the interior with his small Kumalo 'raiding kingdom'. The Ndebele settled first in what is today Lesotho and then moved north to the Marico area of the Transvaal where, in 1836, they were confronted and defeated by the vanguard of the white Voortrekkers. Not long afterwards Mzilikazi crossed the Limpopo into Zimbabwe to forge a coherent and, in military terms, formidable nation from his Ndebele and Sotho followers and the region's resident people (see also Historical Background, page 23).

Though they differ in detail, many Ndebele cultural traditions – the importance placed on kinship ties, concepts of wealth and status, religious belief and so on – are broadly similar to those of the Shona. Where sharp distinctions do occur is in the realm of language: Shona is divided into a number of related dialects (though Karanga draws much from the Nguni), while the Ndebele speak Si'Ndebele, a very different tongue. Contrasts are evident, too, when it comes to social systems. The rural Shona recognize the authority of hereditary chiefs but tend towards small, localized and fairly independent units. Among the Ndebele, on the other hand, the concept of nationhood is somewhat stronger, and class, or caste, based on kinship and the structures of the early Matabele military state, still has its place in the psychology, if not in the organization, of the Ndebele communities in Zimbabwe.

ABOVE: *Casual sociability and relaxation in central Harare.*
OPPOSITE PAGE: *Harare, city of a million people.*

The subject, however, is immensely complex, highly sensitive and increasingly irrelevant. Zimbabwe, after decades of strife, is now a single country, its people bound by common loyalties and aspirations. They are leaving the old ways, and the old animosities, behind them, and they prefer to be regarded simply as Zimbabweans.

Nearly three quarters of the people are involved in subsistence farming. The staple crop is maize; other harvests include groundnuts, millet, sorghum and a variety of root and other vegetables. More and more peasant farmers, however, have been turning to commercial crops, a trend encouraged by the government until 1992, when devastating drought and depleted stockpiles forced the authorities to import huge quantities of maize. Many families keep livestock, most notably goats and cattle (about a seventh of the country is classed as rangeland, and half the national herd belongs to communities practising traditional pastoralism). Cattle remain a symbol of wealth, and are still used widely – for instance, in payment of lobolo (bride price).

## CITIES, TOWNS AND PLACES

By far the largest of Zimbabwe's urban concentrations is Harare. Situated on the Highveld (altitude 1 500 m), the place began life in 1890 as Fort Salisbury, and was known simply as Salisbury until, following independence in 1980, it was renamed in honour of Neharare, a local chieftain who had been buried in the region before the coming of the Europeans.

Harare is a small city by international standards. Though the greater metropolitan area has a population approaching a million, the central district is modest in dimension – a trim, modern, bustling complex of neat-looking buildings and unusually broad thoroughfares that conform to a strict grid (streets run north-south; avenues east-west). The best of the panoramic viewing points, apart from the top floors of the Karigamombe building and some of the other taller office blocks, is the Kopje, a prominent and attractively green-garlanded hillock on the southwestern fringes. The Kopje has been a popular lookout for decades but may, in due course, serve a far grander purpose: it is being considered as the site of new and visually splendid parliamentary buildings.

Among the city's most attractive assets are its flowering trees – the avenues, and in particular those just to the north of the central area, are quite beautifully embowered, especially in springtime (September to November), when the jacarandas display their delicate, feathery, lilac-coloured blooms. Other species are almost as numerous and as lovely: the stately, blood-red African flame trees of summer, for example; the crimson poincianas; the pink, purple and white bauhinias; the poinsettias and, everywhere, the tropical stridency of bougainvillea.

Of particular floral note are, first, the Harare Gardens, a step away from city-centre and a pleasant oasis of lawns, trees, shrubs, beautiful beddings, bandstand (Sunday afternoon concerts provide a touch of Edwardian elegance), open-air theatre, swimming pool, bowling greens, an air of quiet tranquility and lovely lights at Christmas; and, second, the National Botanic Gardens, 4 km to the north of the city and respository of fully 5 000 trees covering, between them, a good proportion of the country's 750 indigenous varieties.

The large and architecturally striking National Gallery, on the southern edge of the Harare Gardens, is the home of contemporary Zimbabwean stone sculpture, a distinctive art form that has been internationally recognized, and acclaimed, since it first began to develop in earnest in the early 1960s. According to the experts, at least five and perhaps seven of the world's top ten sculptor-carvers are Zimbabwean; in the opinion of Newsweek magazine the 'Shona school' is probably the most important artistic phenomenon to have emerged from Africa this century.

Among leading sculptors, some of whose work is on display in the gallery (and in London, Paris and New York) are Sylvestor Mubayi, John Takawira, Thomas Mukorabgwa, Joseph Ndandarika, Nicholas Mukomberanwa and Henry Munyaradzi. All

12

these have been producing, and developing, for the past three decades, their collective hallmark an extraordinary stylistic versatility, though a common impressionistic thread runs through much of the best work – dark, dense, compact stone pieces with a brooding, atavistic, intensely spiritual quality about them.

A new generation of talented artists is now coming to the fore, each with his own style and distinction. The danger, though, is that Shona sculpture may become over-popular. Once it reaches cult status, the accolades and the money may flow too easily, the bandwagon will roll and what has up to now been that rare thing, a wholly original form, could degenerate into plain old airport art.

Other galleries, and schools, around the capital and elsewhere in the country, have a wide variety of stone art on display. Eminently worth visiting is the Chapunga Kraal craft village, located in Harare's Msasa suburb.

Harare boasts some handsome buildings, most impressive of which is probably the 4 000-capacity, gold-panelled International Conference Centre, completed in 1986 and the largest and most sophisticated complex of its kind in Africa. The ultramodern Sheraton next door is one of a range of fine city hotels that includes the five-star, sky-scraping, scoopshaped Monomotapa and the more old-world Meikles. The latter was something of an institution in colonial days, its high-ceilinged lounge, festooned with palms and cooled by punkah-fans, a rendezvous much beloved of three generations of gentleman farmers. That's all gone now, but the new Meikles has more than maintained the standards of excellence in all departments, but especially when it comes to service and cuisine, which is cordon bleu.

Talking of food, there's no such thing as a distinctive Zimbabwean culinary tradition in the sense, say, that one can speak of typically Mexican or Greek fare: hotels and restaurants serve the standard range of dishes, those you'd be able to order in any European city. The local beef, though, is special, as is the Kariba bream, and you have a particularly wide choice of delicious tropical and subtropical fruits. And there are a number of delicacies that can be classed as unusual – crocodile tail, for example (which tastes a bit like crab meat), and different types of venison (ostrich, impala, kudu, eland and so forth).

All this is food for the more affluent. Ordinary Zimbabweans hold to a simpler diet, basic to which is maize-meal ('sadza') garnished with a variety of relishes and, when affordable, accompanied by boiled meat ('nyama') of one sort or another. Oxtail stew is popular; occasional treats include flying termites ('ishwa') and the worms of the mopane tree, both of which are fried – the aroma is delectable, the eating (once you're over the psychological barrier) extremely tasty.

Visitors to Harare with a leisurely day to spare have a number of attractive sightseeing options. A stroll down First Street mall will introduce them to the best of the shops; two blocks away, flanking African Unity Square (where Col. Edward Pennefather, commander of the Pioneer Column, raised the old Union flag on 13 September 1890 and until fairly recently known as Cecil Square) is the Anglican Cathedral of St Mary and All Saints, a dignified, modestly distinguished building whose foundation stone was laid in 1913 and which took just over half a century to complete. A little farther afield are:

▪ The National Museum and Library, noted for its fine collection of rock art and its replica of a Shona village. The MacGregor Geological Museum on Fourth Street will also fill a pleasantly informative hour: it features some intriguing displays of rock samples and gemstones.

▪ The National Archives, on the Borrowdale Road: a beautifully run research centre and repository of a splendid collection of

Africana. Its rarer items include paintings by the much under-valued Thomas Baines and the diaries of David Livingstone.

▨ The famed tobacco auctions, on the edge of the Willowvale industrial area southwest of the city, are held between April and September, and are open to the public three mornings a week. Zimbabwe is one of the world's leading producers of the leaf (of both the Virginia and Burley types). The country's 1 750 commercial tobacco farmers harvest around 120 000 tonnes a year; crops have been excellent, and the prices high, of recent years, and there is an invigorating air of busy optimism on the trading floors of the tobacco exchange.

▨ Among the slightly longer excursions recommended to visitors are those to the Ewanrigg botanical garden (41 km east of the city), which boasts outstanding displays of aloes and cycads, seen at their best perhaps in winter and spring; to Lake Chivero (formerly MacIlwaine) in the west, a pleasantly rural complex of water, parkland and wildlife reserve, popular among bream anglers, watersportsmen, picnickers, and game viewers; and to Mazowe in the north, a place of rolling green hills, lush fields of maize and cotton and of aromatic citrus orchards.

**Bulawayo.** The capital of Matabeleland and Zimbabwe's second city lies at a lower altitude than Harare (1 340 m compared to the latter's 1 483 m) and is generally hotter and a lot drier than its big brother to the northeast. Often much too dry: drought has been something of a constant over the past decade or so (up to 1992 only two out of the preceding 14 years had brought normal rains) and the residents are now determined to do something about the crisis: they are strenuously campaigning to bring water from the Zambezi River 400 km to the northwest. It is estimated that just 90 seconds of the river's immense daily flow will fill all of Bulawayo's yearly needs and irrigate the surrounding farmlands as well.

The cost of such a project, at around Z$2 billion in 1990 terms, intimidates a central government desperately needing to cut its spending, and whose political power base lies more in Mashonaland than in Matabeleland. Bulawayans point out, however, that the city's industries are in the economic vanguard, accounting for, among other things, Z$1,5 billion worth of the country's textile exports, and they argue that such enterprise must be nurtured.

Bulawayo was founded in 1872 by the Ndebele king Lobengula (he called it Gubulawayo, which means 'place of slaughter'), was burnt to the ground in the punitive Matabele War of 1893 and re-established, in the following year, a few kilometres distant (settler houses had already been built on the original site; why the settlement was moved remains a mystery). It is now an attractive, rather spread-out little city of modern though modestly proportioned commercial buildings, jacaranda-lined thoroughfares that are even broader than those of Harare (they were originally designed to allow eight-span wagons to manoeuvre) and a resident population of around half a million, most of whom are of Ndebele stock.

ABOVE: *Harare's famed tobacco auctions. The crop accounts for nearly a fifth of Zimbabwe's export earnings.*

Textiles are perhaps the most prominent segment of an impressively wide industrial spectrum that also encompasses tyre-manufacture, building materials, vehicles, radios and other electronic goods, printing, packaging and food processing. Bulawayo is also the headquarters of Zimbabwe's comparatively sophisticated rail network, and its railways museum, in the suburb of Raylton, is well worth an hour or so of a tourist's time for its turn-of-the-century locomotives and rolling stock.

For much of the year the city tends to look parched, the air dusty, the streets covered by a thin film of Kalahari sand, but the residential gardens are lovely and parts of the wider central area remain gloriously green throughout the seasons. Bulawayo's 'green lung' flanks the Amatsheumhlope River that runs through suburb and city; Central Park boasts tall palms and other magnificent arboreal species, and an exquisite rose garden; Centenary Park – venue of the 1953 Rhodes Centenary Exhibition – has emerald lawns, shady trees, brightly flowering shrubs, aviary, game enclosure and, at its edge, a lively little theatre and the National History Museum.

This last has some fascinating exhibits, among them artefacts from Great Zimbabwe and other ruins; a 75 000-item mammal collection (the southern hemisphere's most extensive); the 2 000-year-old egg of an extinct Madagascan bird (said to be the inspiration for Sinbad's giant Roc) and a mounted elephant that stands over three metres tall.

ABOVE: *The graceful town of Mutare, gateway to the Eastern Highlands. To the north lies Nyanga, to the south, Vumba.*

Features of special tourist appeal in the general area are the Mzilikazi art and craft centre, which produces fine sculptural work; and Chipangali, an orphanage for sick and abandoned animals, some of whom are returned to the wild.

Sixteen kilometres outside Bulawayo are the walled terraces of the Kame Ruins, second only to Great Zimbabwe in size, once the headquarters of the Rosvi royal dynasty and still a place of profound mystical relevance to the Shona people.

And, of course, there are the Matobo Hills and national park to the south, a place of massive, immensely ancient granite formations – crags, whalebacks and domes – and of caves and cliff faces adorned with the paintings and engravings of those most superlative of prehistoric artists, the San, or Bushmen. The domes and whalebacks are known locally as dwalas; the word 'Matobo' means 'bald heads', a name said to have been conferred by Mzilikazi in one of his more whimsical moments: the landscape reminded him of an assembly of his aged councillors.

Here, in these mysterious, hauntingly beautiful hills, the Karangan oracles recieved the words of Mwari, the all-powerful god; here the great soldier-king Mzilikazi left his mark and was buried, and it was to this place that the Ndebele warriors retreated to make their last, defiant stand against the white invaders. And here, too, at a succession of dignified indabas, Cecil Rhodes made peace with their chiefs. Rhodes died near Cape Town in March 1902, but his wishes were that he be buried in the place he loved best. His body was taken 2 000 kilometres to the north into the wilderness of the Matobos, and the 'immense and brooding spirit' was finally laid to rest in a simple grave carved from the summit of a hill he had named World's View.

**Mutare.** Formerly known as Umtali, this graceful little town, gateway to the Eastern Highlands, lies beneath Christmas Pass in the warm and fertile valley of the Sakubva River in one of the most scenically spectacular settings imaginable: it is almost entirely enclosed by mountains of unrivalled grandeur.

Mutare, which officially became a city in 1971, has a population of something approaching 100 000 and a local economy based on the products of the prosperous Manicaland region (tea, tobacco, timber, livestock), on industrial activity (oil refining, motor assembly, textiles, clothing and leather goods, food processing) and on tourism. To the north is the Nyanga national park; to the south the beautiful Vumba uplands.

The town complements its setting: it is attractively laid out, its streets and suburbs graced by a breathtaking profusion of flowering trees and shrubs – jacaranda in springtime, the crimson glory of flame in high summer and bougainvillea, it seems, everywhere and at every time of the year.

Mutare also serves as the exit point into Mozambique, the highway east leading down into the humid coastal plain and thence to the port of Beira. In older, more peaceful times Zimbabweans poured across the border for their casual seaside weekends at Mr Brito's Estoril cabanas, drawn by the delicious prawns, the acrid wine and the good Laurentina beer of a territory that belonged to, and was fairly heavily populated by, the

the former, 164 km from the latter) now has a solid industrial base that includes the railway marshalling yards and a variety of manufacturing enterprises, among which shoe-making – 10 million pairs a year – remains prominent. Mining also contributes to its prosperity: early Karangan miners worked the earth for gold, and the metal is still found in the area, but its other minerals – prominent among them asbestos, limestone, tungsten – are now rather more important.

Gweru is also known for its military connections: an Empire air force training school was established here during the Second World War (cloudless skies, wind-free air and the flattish terrain made it an ideal choice) to be followed, a few years later, by an infantry school.

**Masvingo**, capital of the Masvingo province in the south, started life as Fort Victoria, second of the military-colonial encampments established by Cecil Rhodes's Pioneer Column on its long journey to Harare in 1890. It then became an important staging post and the centre of considerable mining, ranching and farming activity, all of which still play a significant role in the region's economy.

So too does tourism. To the south lies Mutirikwe (formerly Kyle), third largest of Zimbabwe's lakes and a pleasantly developed recreational area and game park. Among the animals introduced in the latter are white rhino, giraffe and several kinds of buck; hippo wallow along the shallow shores, and a growing number of bird species are making their homes on the many islands. The 63-metre-high dam and 90 km² man-made lake were created to supply water to the massive Lowveld sugar and citrus estates. The lake dried up completely during the savage drought of 1991-92.

Some 32 km to the west of Masvingo is the Mushandike sanctuary (see page 23); to the southwest is the region's biggest tourist attraction: Great Zimbabwe. Although the place, now a declared World Heritage Site, had been occupied in the early centuries of the first millennium, the three main stone complexes – hill, great enclosure and valley – were built between 1 000 and 1 200 AD, the Karangan state flourishing until the 15th century, when it went into sudden decline (see Historical Background, page 23). In its heyday its kings held immense power and wealth, derived from the gold of the region and from trading relations that went far beyond southern Africa, in one period extending as far as central Asia, India and China.

The few glass beads and pottery unearthed by archaeologists attest to links with distant lands, and they led early European travellers, romanticists almost to a man, to dream of ancient Ophir and of Great Zimbabwe's exotic beginnings, but the most important of their finds – eight carvings of the famed 'Zimbabwe Bird' – are, like the entire complex, of local origin. Fashioned from soft soapstone and standing over 30 cm high, they are stylized representations of the fish eagle, sacred to the Hungwe group of the Karanga people. The bird is now one of Zimbabwe's national symbols, featuring in the coat of arms and on coins.

TOP: *Gweru, the largest of Zimbabwe's midland towns.*
ABOVE: *Rural women of the Masvingo region.*

Portuguese, but the wars of liberation fought in both countries and the vicious civil strife that later erupted in Mozambique all but put an end to such frivolity. Progress towards peace has been made but the route remains potentially hazardous.

**Gweru.** The fourth of Zimbabwe's cities and capital of the country's midlands, Gweru (formerly Gwelo) was a ranching and agricultural centre until the late 1930s, when the first of its industries, a shoe factory, was established. The town, on the main highway between Harare and Bulawayo (it is 275 km from

Great Zimbabwe is the largest and most impressive of some 1 500 stone ruins scattered around the country. Apart from those of Kame (see page 15) and one or two others, most are extremely modest in comparison. The monument is open to the public during the day; on site is a fascinating little museum and an aloe garden that is bright with colour in June and July.

**Kwekwe** stands astride the main highway almost exactly half way between Harare and Bulawayo. Founded as the military fort of Sebakwe in the 1890s, its name was changed to Que Que after the river that flows nearby (the word is onomatopoeic, representing the croaking of frogs that live in and around the waters).

The town, now an attractive little place of wide, lawn-fringed and shady streets, owed its early prosperity to two outcrops of gold-bearing rock, the Globe and the Phoenix. The claims were combined in 1894 to sustain one of southern Africa's most lucrative small mines, and other workings were opened up in the area. The National Gold Mining Museum of Zimbabwe, unusual centrepiece of which is a 'paper house' – a prefabricated affair imported in 1894 to serve as the Globe & Phoenix's manager – welcomes visitors to the town.

Much later, vast deposits of high-grade iron ore were discovered in the region, and in 1942 a brand new town, Redcliff, made its appearance in the hills 14 km south of Kwekwe. Redcliff is a trim little place of some 25 000 residents, most of them dependent for their living on the giant Zimbabwe Iron and Steel Company (Zisco) parastatal enterprise. The plant is able to turn out a million tonnes of liquid steel each year; most of the ore now comes from Buchwa, about 180 km to the southeast.

The Kwekwe region produces a range of cultivated crops, among them winter cerials, maize, coffee, cotton, citrus – and barley, which sustains a huge malting plant supplying the country's major (indeed only) brewery.

Also in the general area is the Sebakwe recreational park, a lovely place of lake and gentle countryside which, although not proclaimed as a reserve, nurtures kudu and impala and a variety of birds attracted to the placid waters.

**Kadoma.** Formerly known as Gatooma, this modestly pleasant centre of some 60 000 inhabitants was founded in 1906 as a railway siding on the line between Bulawayo and Harare and it, too, grew up around the gold diggings (in this case the Cam & Motor mine). Other minerals – chrome, nickel, magnesite – also occur in the vicinity, but it draws most of its wealth from the cotton fields of the countryside and the textile mill in town.

**Zvishavane** (formerly Shabani), on the lowland grasslands between Masvingo and Bulawayo, is a fairly substantial town of around 35 000 people and the centre of the largest asbestos-producing complex in the southern hemisphere.

**Hwange**, in the far west, 50 km from the Victoria Falls, also owes its existence to the mineral wealth of the area – in this case

coal, originally exploited by a German trader and prospector named Albert Giese, who had heard from the locals of 'black stones that burned'. A little later, around the turn of the century, the Wankie colliery began working one of Africa's largest and richest deposits. The town has a population of about 40 000; the mine-shafts, open-cast workings and attendant industrial development have of course disfigured parts of a countryside that was once Mzilikazi's favourite hunting preserve. To the south sprawls the Hwange national park, one of the world's grandest wilderness areas (see page 20).

**Chinoyi** (formerly Sinoia), 115 km northwest of Harare and a town of some 30 000 residents, serves as the centre of flourishing farmlands (tobacco, maize, cattle) and of the copper and chrome mines of the area. Its major claim to fame, however, is the nearby, labyrinthine cave complex – in reality a giant sinkhole with a number of supplementary passages and chambers. The hole is filled with motionless, intensely blue, iridescent water. A magical place.

ABOVE: *Carpets of multicoloured cosmos give glorious colour to the Zimbabwean countryside during autumn.*

**Marondera** (formerly Marandellas), on the Mutare road 74 km from Harare, is a leading educational centre, location of a number of prestigious private schools. It's also the hub of a particularly productive farming region that encompasses beef and dairy cattle pastures, tobacco lands, fields of grain, timber plantations – and vineyards (the area has pioneered the country's young and promising wine industry). The attractive town boasts its own racecourse, one of the country's prettiest and oldest.

LEFT: *Kapenta sun-drying in the Kariba area. About 15 000 tons of these small, sardine-like fish are harvested each year.*

**Victoria Falls.** The township, with a permanent population of 10 000, is of course a major tourist centre. The railway bridge across the Zambezi east of the falls was completed in 1905 – a stunning feat of engineering and a standing monument to Cecil Rhodes's driving ambition (the project had been initiated before his death in 1902). On the opposite (Zambian) side of the river is the town of Livingstone.

Victoria Falls township comprised little more than a scatter of storage and rest huts, a trading store, the grand old Victoria Falls Hotel and a few curio outlets until about three decades ago, when it really began to develop. Today there are half-a-dozen or so hotels of international standard, casinos, restaurants, shopping centre and international airport. Visitors spend their days drinking in the grandeur and beauty of the thundering waters, exploring the river and its banks (the more intrepid on foot or by raft, the less so by sunset cruise and light aircraft); playing golf (wildlife is a feature of the fairways), touring the national park and, in the evening, dining, wining, gambling, being entertained. Special drawcards are the multi-cultural craft village, a splendid exposition of traditional lifestyles, custom, architecture, ornamentaion, music and drama; and the crocodile ranch, which contains around 2 000 of the giant reptiles.

**Kariba.** The town, nestling among the hillocks that overlook the dam wall, was built in the 1950s to house construction and engineering workers – many of them Italians – employed on the wall and, later, in the hydro-electric power station.

The wall comprises a 126-metre-high, 21-metre-thick concrete arch that runs 600 metres across the narrow gorge from one bank of the Zambezi to the other. The six sluice gates are capable of discharging 9 400 cumecs of floodwater; the power plant, its giant turbines and alternators are housed in a massive chamber carved out of solid rock. The project, a grand though, as it turned out, too-optimistic symbol of federal unity (see page 26), was officially opened by Queen Elizabeth the Queen Mother on 17 May 1960.

Kariba township is a neat little centre, its 'best area' the Heights, where there are some smart houses, a shopping complex, supermarket, bakery, and the eye-catching church (it is an 'open' circular building featuring a series of archways instead of walls). Not far from town is the Kariba crocodile farm, to which visitors are welcomed (some handsome leather goods are on sale in the curio shop). Until fairly recently the lake, 40 km at its widest, 280 km long, 5 180 km² in extent, ranked as the world's largest man-made reservoir. When full, it contains 160 thousand million cubic metres of water, and to skirt its perimeter involves an extensive 4 000-km trek.

So much for statistics: they say much about the size and scope of the hydro-electric scheme, but tell you nothing of the wild beauty of the place, of its islands and inlets, and of the resorts and marinas that make of Kariba one of Africa's finest leisure areas. Nor do they hint of the romance, mystery and drama of its beginnings – the displacement of 50 000 Tonga people and the anger of Nyaminyami, the River God; the unprecedented floods that killed 17 workers (altogether, more than 70 died during the four-year construction period) and which threatened to destroy the dam; and of the myriad animals that were trapped on the shrinking patches of dry land by the young lake's rising waters. Most of the game – 5 000 head in all – was rescued by rangers during the huge and heroic relocation scheme known as 'Operation Noah'.

The lake, its shores and their surrounds are now an attractively developed playground for the fisherman, the watersportsman, yachtsman and laid-back holidaymaker. The waters are usually placid (but not always so: sudden wind-storms can whip up dangerously large waves) and, enriched by the dead vegetation of drowned forests and the 'Kariba weed' infestation, they sustain more than 40 freshwater species, including the nutritious sardine-type kapenta, fat bream, chissa, vundu (barbel) and the feisty tigerfish so sought after by serious anglers. Among the more favoured venues are Fothergill and Spurwing islands (each has its safari camp), the busy little harbour of Andora, near the gorge (yachts, houseboats, fishing rigs, charter cruisers), and the string of marinas and resorts along the lake's southern shore. The most attractive of the hotels, in architectural terms, is probably the Mediterranean-style Caribbea Bay. The popular Kariba car ferry, 'Sealion', is based at Andora and makes regular return trips to Mlibizi harbour at the western end of the lake.

The lake area is also a wildlife paradise: hippo and crocodile abound; the shore vegetation, that between the tide-lines, is a rich mix of aquatic and terrestial grasses that attracts elephant and rhino, giraffe, buffalo and a host of other animals. A number of extensive parks and safari areas have been established around and near the lake.

# WILD KINGDOM

To those who want to see wildlife at its grandest and most prolific, Zimbabwe offers a veritable treasurehouse of riches.

More than 12 percent of the country's land is taken up by proclaimed parks and safari areas, the habitats ranging from dry Kalahari sandveld in the west through the woodland savannah and open grasslands of the moister areas to the deep-green mountain forests and heaths of the eastern uplands. All in all a superb diversity.

Conservation of wildlife – and the term encompasses the protection of all forms of life in its indigenous state, including the trees and the shrubs and grasses (though the larger mammals perhaps have a special place in the scheme) – ranks high on the government's list of priorities. And understandably so: Zimbabwe's natural heritage is a priceless asset, worth preserving as a gift to future generations and, more immediately, because it is capable of earning the country a great deal of desperately needed foreign exchange.

In overall control is the Department of Parks and Wildlife Management, a division of government that has chalked up a fine record. The parks are beautifully run, both for visitors (accommodation and facilities are of the highest standard) and for the residents: conservation techniques are advanced, meticulously applied and, for the most part, highly successful, most

obviously so in the management of black rhino and elephant. The former, endangered elsewhere, now number a healthy 1 500, the largest such population in the world (though it remains under threat from poachers, especially in the rugged wilderness of the Zambezi valley); the latter 50 000, which is probably more than their habitats can comfortably cope with. The national elephant herd, two-fifths of which finds sanctuary in the Hwange national park and half the remainder in the Zambezi valley complex, has steadily increased in size over the past decade or so – in marked contrast to the situation in many other African countries, where in some cases the numbers have been depleted to the point of regional extinction.

For all that, though, Zimbabwe's wildlife has been and is under severe pressure, mainly from human encroachment – simply because the country has a rapidly growing population, but finite resources. To cope with the strains, a far-sighted piece of

**RIGHT:** *A 'safari boat', owned by the Bumi Hills Lodge, at rest in one of Lake Kariba's remoter inlets.*
**BELOW:** *First light on the still waters of Lake Kariba.*

legislation, the Parks and Wildlife Bill, was enacted in the mid-1970s and its effects have, by and large, exceeded all expectations. The act enables ranchers, farmers, village communities and others who occupy private and communal land to manage the habitats and use them for gain (by game-ranching and through controlled hunting, for example, and by culling excess animals for meat). The result is a double benefit: on the one hand many Zimbabweans are receiving a direct reward, in either cash or kind, from their efforts, and, on the other, the environment in general and its wildlife in particular are being sustained. Zimbabwe's major wilderness areas are:

**Hwange national park.** Situated in the far west, this prince of parks covers nearly 15 000 km² of heat-blistered Kalahari sand country – grassland plains with scattered bush and trees – and is reported to have a greater variety and density of wildlife than any other area in the world. The northern section is characterized by rocky outcrops, extensive teak forests and mopane woodlands, but for the rest the terrain is fairly flat and open, which is of course ideal for game-viewing. The rest-camps, though, are in the north: the southern segment – most of the park – remains a pristine wilderness in which the animals are left virtually undisturbed.

Hwange has no perennial streams, but there is plenty of water in the pans and pump-supplied waterholes, and these sources nurture the great herds of elephant, the rhino (both black and white), the giraffe, zebra, buffalo, sable, roan and other antelope, lion, leopard (Hwange is sanctuary to 25 types

ABOVE: *Rukomechi bush camp lies alongside the Zambezi River upstream of Mana Pools national park.*
OPPOSITE, ABOVE: *Zimbabwe's parks and wilderness areas are well served by private safari camps. Here, visitors enjoy an alfresco meal at Ivory Lodge, near Hwange.*
OPPOSITE, BELOW: *Game-viewers at Matusadona park.*

of predator) and the more than 400 bird species. The elephant are more prolific in the dry season: during the rains many of them migrate across the border into northern Botswana.

There are three major camps – Main, Sinamatella and Robins – and a number of smaller ones, linked togather by some 480 km of game-viewing drives along which there are picnic spots and viewsites, most of which overlook waterholes. At Main Camp you can observe the game by moonlight – an unforgettable experience. On the park's north-eastern boundary is the thatched and luxurious Hwange Safari Lodge; Ivory Lodge is also a much-favoured venue; altogether, there are five hotels and an airport within short driving distance of the park.

**Victoria Falls and Zambezi national parks.** The area immediately around the falls is a proclaimed national park, created to preserve among other things the magnificent rainforest, a magical place rich in animal and, especially, in plant life. Falls and forest are recognized as a World Heritage Site.

Next door is the 54 000-ha Zambezi national park, haven to elephant, buffalo and, in the riverine area, a superb array of birds. There are about 130 km of game-viewing roads and, for the more energetic, a 50-km trail leading along the river-bank. The main camp offers two-bedroomed lodges; anglers have the choice of three fishing camps, one on Kandahar Island.

**Chizarira national park** covers 192 000 hectares of rugged hill terrain – the Zambezi escarpment – to the east of Lake Kariba and, although it has an abundance of animals and birds, does not play host to a great many visitors: it is remote, accessible only to four-wheel-drive vehicles, and one needs permission to enter the area. Once in, though, you're rewarded by a splendid landscape of mountain and deep ravine and a wildlife complement that includes elephant, black rhino and buffalo. Among the park's birds are the crowned eagle, bat hawk, Livingstone's flycatcher, racket-tailed roller and the elusive Taita falcon.

**Matusadona national park**, the second of the Kariba region's three proclaimed areas, fringes the lake and extends over almost 1 500 km² of wild escarpment countryside. The undulating bush-covered hills support fine populations of rhino, elephant and buck, and are crossed by wilderness trails and one or two rough roads. This is the 'real' Africa, huge, untouched. The Ume River runs along the western boundary, the Senyati and its precipitous gorge along the eastern.

Most popular part of the park is its shoreline, an aquatic wilderness of bays, inlets, river estuaries and, offshore, attractive little islands that are much favoured by fishermen, birdwatchers and lovers of nature at its most tranquil. Visitors stay at one or other of the three exclusive camps (in nicely appointed self-contained chalets), at the Tashinga camping ground or at the luxurious Bumi Hills Safari Lodge on the western edge of the park.

**Charara safari area** hugs the lake's eastern shores and offers excellent game-viewing (beware the lion and elephant that loiter along the dirt road) and fishing. Charara has one rest-camp, Nyanyana, through which elephant often pass. Farther down the Zambezi, to the east, is the:

**Mana Pools national park** which, together with the associated safari areas of Chewore (3 390 km²), Dande (523 km²), Urungwe (2 870 km²), Sapi (1 180 km²) and Doma (764 km²), is a declared World Heritage Site.

This is the Zambezi valley in all its rugged splendour, one of the last of Africa's true wilderness areas. It's not the healthiest of regions – the malarial mosquito, the tsetse fly and the bilharzia snail are all-too-common residents of this comparatively low-lying and humid place – but for all that it has a very special place on the discerning visitor's itinerary.

Over the millennia the sluggish northward-flowing river has deposited rich alluvial soils, and has created pools and channels in which water seasonally collects, and the moisture and the lush vegetation – the sweet grasses, the acacia and mopane – attract vast numbers of game animals, among them elephant (about 12 000 of them), great herds of zebra and buffalo, lion, leopard, hyaena and Cape hunting dog.

A pristine paradise, but one under threat. There has been talk of damming the river farther downstream, thus permanently

inundating the floodplains. Many of the rare black rhino have been destroyed by poachers, who continue to operate with deadly persistence despite the most strenuous counter-measures. Schemes to eradicate the tsetse fly will, if undertaken, open up the region to cattle – perhaps the quickest and most efficient way of destroying the environment. And so on.

But, for the time being, this splendid stretch of the Zambezi valley remains a wild kingdom without parallel.

Accommodation in Mana Pools is limited to two smallish camps: access is by four-wheel-drive and light aircraft; most game-viewers put up at Kariba's smart hotels.

**Nyanga Mountains national park**, at the northern end of the Eastern Highlands, is an entirely different world from that of the Zambezi valley, a high (2 000 – 2 300-m), 33 000-ha expanse of rugged terrain renowned more for its splendid scenery than for its wildlife, though it is home to a fascinating array of small montane animals and a wide variety of bird life.

The landscape is indeed stunning: the hills, often mantled by dense plantations and indigenous forests, fall to deep and lovely

valleys and rise to high and beautiful peaks (Inyangani, 2 539 m, is Zimbabwe's loftiest). Of the several waterfalls in the park, the Pungwe and Nyangombe are the most spectacular.

This is a prime holiday region, well served by vacation cottages, lodges, excellent hotels (among them the celebrated Troutbeck Inn), golf courses and dams that are stocked by Zimbabwe's largest trout hatchery.

Just to the south is the Mtarazi Falls national park, proclaimed to preserve the beauty of the waterfall, the misty heaths, the mountain forests and their denizens, among them the shy samango monkey, the tree civet and the stately crowned eagle. The falls, at the southern extremity of the Nyanga mountains, are Zimbabwe's highest: they tumble over the rim to plunge, in two stages, fully 760 metres to the beautiful Honde valley below.

**Vumba and Bunga Forest botanical reserves.** These two patches of upland forest country, the former a modest 200 ha, the latter 1 560 ha, preserve the rich indigenous plant life – and the birds – of the Vumba mountains. The Vumba reserve encloses a 76-ha garden of magical beauty.

**Chimanimani national park** covers almost all of the dramatic Chimanimani mountain range in the southern segment of the Eastern Highlands. This is a lovely land of craggy krantzes, deep valleys and a myriad perennial streams, of forest, heath and grassland, of proteas, ericas and everlastings, the whole combining to recall the distinctive floral character of South Africa's western Cape region. A lovely, twisting and often misty road links the villages of Chimanimani and Chipinge.

Largest of the park's animals are the occasional eland and sable antelope; klipspringer clamber precariously over rocky outcrops; the shy blue duiker can sometimes be seen; baboons are common. The similarities to the south-western Cape are carried through to the avian life: among familiar species here are the sugarbirds and the malachite sunbird.

A short distance to the west is the Chimanimani eland sanctuary, an 18-km² patch of mountain terrain that contains the magnificent Bridal Veil falls, together with waterbuck, zebra and a remnant population of eland, the only large antelope to thrive among pine plantations. Farther south, beyond the town of Chipinge, is the Chirinda Forest botanical reserve, a splendid, almost 1 000-ha expanse of evergreen montane forest (giant fig trees, ironwood and red mahogany, including a 66-m specimen, the tallest in Zimbabwe); a dense undergrowth of mosses, ferns and creepers; elusive forest birds and animals and, during the rains, an array of graceful butterflies.

**Gonarezhou national park** lies in low, hot, flattish mopane country on the southeastern border with Mozambique and close to South Africa's renowned Kruger park. Indeed many of the larger game animals move freely over the borders; the Kruger's elephant and eland, in particular, migrate seasonally. The wildlife, which can perhaps be seen at its best in the area of the Chipinda Pools, is prolific, encompassing among others black rhino, hippo, oribi, klipspringer, the rare Lichtenstein's hartebeest, suni, nyala and, of course, elephant. The major river is the Save; also prominent is the Runde, which is flanked by dramatic red-sandstone cliffs and which, curiously enough, is home to two marine species (swordfish and tarpan) as well as to bream, tigerfish and the 'living fossil' lungfish.

Gonarezhou, 5 000 km² in extent, is potentially one of southern Africa's finest game parks, but it has its problems: the vegetation has suffered from bush-burning (part of the tsetse fly control programme) and from damage caused by the over-large elephant population; the waters of the two major rivers are being siphoned off for irrigation; and bands of poachers, most of whom cross over from strife-torn Mozambique, have been decimating the herds. Still, the park remains a magnificent wilderness and, once the difficulties have been overcome, may well rival mighty Hwange in its splendour.

**Mushandike sanctuary**, some 30 km southwest of the town of Masvingo, is a multi-purpose area that combines game conservation, game farming, recreation, research and education (Zimbabwe's Natural Resources College is located within its bounds). The hill-enclosed Mushandike dam is much favoured by anglers (black bass, tilapia, bream); wildlife includes white rhino, zebra and buck species.

**Matobo national park.** Part of the grand Matobo range of hills near Bulawayo (see page 15) has been proclaimed as a 43 000-ha haven for rhino and giraffe, zebra and an impressive number of leopard, though these solitary cats tend to hide themselves away in the rocky vastness and are seldom seen. The Matobo Hills are renowned for their birds of prey, and most notably for the black eagle, a species that builds its enormous nest on the highest and most inaccessible ledges.

# HISTORICAL BACKGROUND

South-central Africa was home to different Stone Age communities from about half a million years ago, small bands of hunter-gatherers who, over the millennia, refined their tool- and weapon-making skills and from whom the San (Bushmen) eventually emerged to dominate the sunlit spaces, and to decorate the caves and granite cliff faces with their marvellous paintings. There are more than 6 000 recorded rock-art sites in Zimbabwe and, one suspects, a great many more remain to be discovered.

The first tentative waves of the taller, darker-skinned Bantu-speakers, people who kept livestock and cultivated the land, who had learnt to mine and work with iron, crossed the Zambezi a little over 2 000 years ago, gaining numbers and strength over the following centuries to submerge, and in many cases to displace, the scattered clans of San.

The ancestors of the modern Shona came later, some time in the 10th century it is thought, and settled on the great grassland plains that border on the Kalahari, fanning out from there to spread themselves over a much wider area. Culturally they were far in advance of their predecessors: they developed their own, rather elegant style of pottery; they mined gold, which they traded with the Arab merchants of the east coast, and they knew how to build with stone. It was these people, the early Shona-Karanga, who erected the first of the structures that became known as Great Zimbabwe (see page 16).

**The golden empire**

Between the 11th and 15th centuries Great Zimbabwe functioned, and under a succession of powerful kings continued to develop in ever grander fashion, as the centre of an empire that stretched from today's Botswana east to the coast and from the Zambezi to the Limpopo.

Not that the power of the kings went unchallenged. The dominant section of the Karanga, the Rosvi, had to contend with other invaders from the north, and as a consequence created a highly disciplined military monarchy, recognized and revered as the Mwene Mutapa (corrupted by later colonists to 'Monomotapa'). The kingdom was sustained for close on three centuries by its gold mines, by a wealth of cattle, by fertile farmlands and by traffic in precious metals and ivory.

Then, some time in the 1400s, the centre of Rosvi power shifted to the north, and the Karangan empire slid into decline. One can only guess at the reasons for this abrupt change of fortune, but it is known that there were internal feuds – between the monarchy and some of the more influential chieftains – which must have strained the political and social fabric to breaking point. Moreover, a too-large concentration of people and consequent over-grazing could well have impoverished the land. And, most important of all, mining methods weren't sophisticated enough to enable gold to be extracted from any depth, and the city-state's prime source of wealth became depleted. However that may be, the central authority was weakened, allowing various Shona groups to create powerful semi-autonomous regimes.

Early in the 16th century the Karanga made their first contact with the Portuguese, who had established a commercial presence at Sofala and other east-coast points strategic to the lucrative Indian trade. Portuguese merchants, missionaries and frontiersmen had also ventured up the lower Zambezi valley and, more tentatively, into the land of the Karanga. There, Arab influence was still strong, the indigenous people hostile, and Christian pathfinders such as Antonio Fernandes and the Jesuit missionary Gonçalo da Silviera, and a number of military expeditions launched later, made little headway.

During the following three centuries the interior regions were riven by dynastic rivalry, principally between the Changamire kings of the Rosvi group and those of the Mutapa state. In the event the Rosvi were able to maintain a vague kind of authority over much of what is now Zimbabwe until, in the late 1700s and early 1800s, it collapsed in the face of successive invasions by Nguni warrior groups (notably the Angoni) from the south.

The abrupt and total demise of the Rosvi empire coincided with the most vigorous of the incursions, that of Mzilikazi's Ndebele (see page 11).

ABOVE: *The 19th-century missionary, doctor and explorer David Livingstone, whose Zambezi odyssey captured the imagination of the western world.*

### The Ndebele kingdom

Pushed northwards from his base near Kuruman by the advancing Voortrekkers, Mzilikazi crossed the Limpopo in the late 1830s to found a powerful military state centred on Mhlahlandela, the capital he established to the south of the rugged Matobo Hills. His relatives by blood and marriage, and the most trusted of his indunas, were placed in authority over outlying settlements; aggressive Ndebele war parties regularly raided neighbouring territories, on occasion penetrating as far north as the Zambezi River.

During Mzilikazi's violently autocratic 30-year reign the first Europeans – hunters, ivory traders, explorers, seekers of gold – made their cautious way from the south into the lands beyond the Limpopo River. So too did the men of God, among them the great missionary-explorer David Livingstone and his father-in-law, Robert Moffat. The latter had befriended Mzilikazi at Kuruman before the Ndebele exodus, and now received the king's blessing on the first mission station to be established in Matabeleland (at Inyati, in 1859).

Livingstone was not closely involved in the politics of the time. His vision was broader – he aimed to end the pernicious slave trade by opening up Africa to Christianity and commerce – and he personally had little influence on the fortunes of the Ndebele kingdom and its neighbours, but his travels did fire the imagination of the English-speaking world, directing a lot of popular interest towards the unknown interior of central Africa.

Livingstone had set out in the late 1840s on the first of several exploratory expeditions, the greatest a four-year odyssey that took him to Luanda (on Angola's Atlantic coast) and from there inland along the Zambezi to its estuary at Quelimane on the Indian Ocean and, in 1855, to the Victoria Falls. The journey, made by ox-wagon and on foot, covered 9 000 km of rugged African terrain, and it inspired other explorers – Burton, Speke and Baker among them – to unravel more of the mysteries of what Victorians liked to call the Dark Continent. Still other travellers had different motives, and sent a more specific message to the world: men such as Karl Mauch and the self-taught artist Thomas Baines returned with stories (vastly exaggerated, as it turned out) of the land of Ophir and its fabulous riches.

Mzilikazi died in 1868, to be succeeded by his second son Lobengula, 34 years old at the time of his coronation and a leader of quality who, among other things, continued to extend the hand of friendship to visiting Europeans, among them Frederick Courteney Selous, the hunter and inspiration of Rider Haggard's novel Alan Quartermain.

### Cecil Rhodes's scheme

Ndebele attitudes began to harden, however, from the late 1870s. European politicians were turning their attention to the trans-Limpopo territories; concession-seekers were a constant irritant (a British government party had descended on Gubulawayo, the new Ndebele capital, as early as 1877); the Portuguese were attempting to reassert ancient claims to the interior; the Boers of the Transvaal were looking north for yet more 'living space', and Lobengula increasingly , and justifiably, felt himself under siege. At one point he was led to complain, bitterly, of intruders who came 'like wolves ... and make roads in my country'.

All this was part, albeit a relatively small one, of the so-called 'Scramble for Africa', a colossal exercise in colonial cupidity born of rivalry between the industrialized states in Europe. Powerful interests were invloved, the political stakes were high (by the end of the century the continental map had been redrawn, arbitrarily and with a wholly cynical disregard for the indigenous peoples). Leading contender in the south-central African arena was Cecil John Rhodes, the immensely wealthy South African mining magnate, politician and empire-builder whose vision encompassed, among other things, an Imperial highway from the Cape to Cairo.

Rhodes believed in the golden treasurehouse of the 'Far North', and was convinced that the creation of a 'second Witwatersrand' would tip the balance of power away from the Boers of the Transvaal in favour of the English-speaking communities of southern Africa. The new territory, he foresaw, should be part of the British Empire but, because he had an innate distrust of the meddlesome politicians of Whitehall (and because he was personally ambitious), was adamant that it should be allowed to govern itself.

In 1888 Rhodes's agent, Charles Rudd, extracted valuable mineral rights from Lobengula (it is doubtful whether the latter knew precisely what he was signing away). Rhodes then formed the British South Africa Company which, in the following year, received from Queen Victoria a royal charter conferring on it extensive political, administrative and economic powers in the designated lands.

In 1890 the BSA Company recruited and equipped a force of policemen and settlers to occupy Mashonaland, the region to the north of the Ndebele kingdom, and on 13 September, after a slow and troubled trek to and across Zimbabwe's Highveld, the Pioneer Column raised the flag at Fort Salisbury, now Harare.

## Settlement and war

The BSA Company, though commercial in its basic intent, was an independent political state in all but name. Its charter empowered it to levy taxes, build roads and railways, make treaties with African chieftains, dispense justice, mint coinage, maintain its own civil service, armed forces and police – and go to war. Which it did three years after the occupation. Gold, and more territory, were its principal objectives, and the vast Ndebele domains to the southwest were a tempting prize. Ndebele incursions into the Fort Victoria (now Masvingo) area and a skirmish with Company forces provided the pretext, and in mid-1893 Dr L.S. Jameson, the Company's administrator in what was already being informally referred to as Rhodesia, decided to invade Lobengula's kingdom.

By November it was all over. In a 14-week campaign the Company's well-armed and equipped 900-man force, organized in three mounted columns and supported by some Bechuanaland Border Police and African auxiliaries, advanced into Matabeleland, dispersed the Ndebele regiments, burnt Gubulawayo to the ground, put Lobengula to flight, suffered a sharp reverse on the banks of the Shangani River (a largish patrol, led by Major Allan Wilson, was wiped out) and went on to occupy the region. The king died not long afterwards, of smallpox, near Kamativi to the northwest.

Encouraged by the 'pacification' of Matabeleland, more settlers arrived in search of gold and, increasingly, of ranches and farms. The Company obliged them by expropriating much of the new territory, allocating 10 500 km² of arid border countryside as an Ndebele 'reserve'.

The pattern of the future – the maintenance of a system akin in many ways to the 'separate development' structures of successive South African governments – had been set. During the first eight decades of the century the white settlers enjoyed legal right to vast acres, while the African peoples were confined to the generally poorer tribal trust lands.

In 1896 the Ndebele, angered by their loss, by the devastation of their herds in the rinderpest epidemic, and by the imposition of forced labour practices, rebelled against the new authority. The moment seemed opportune: Jameson ('Dr Jim') and most of his police were away on their hare-brained and in

ABOVE: *Cecil Rhodes, mining magnate and empire-builder. His British South Africa Company inaugurated the country's ninety-year-long colonial era.*

the event disastrous raid into the Transvaal. Many of the Shona clans joined in the revolt.

The settlers, however, went into laager and managed to hold out until the arrival of military reinforcements. The uprising was crushed; Rhodes personally negotiated peace with the Ndebele at a series of indabas, or conferences, in the Matobo Hills, and in due course the Shona also laid down their arms.

## Colonial home rule

The country began to develop in earnest following the completion, in 1897, of the railway from South Africa to Bulawayo and, two years later, of the line between Salisbury and the Portuguese East African port of Beira.

Southern Rhodesia (the prefix was added in 1911), it soon transpired, was anything but a new El Dorado, but the gold deposits were nevertheless rich enough to become the mainstay of a flourishing economy that also drew strength from other minerals – coal, chrome and asbestos among them – and from the fruits of the fertile land. Golden harvests of tobacco, in particular, began to contribute substantially to exports from the first years of the century.

There was also modest movement on the white political front. The settlers had received a measure of representation in a legislative assembly established in 1898, but the BSA Company, even though it proved a financial failure (it never once declared a dividend to shareholders), continued to exercise autocratic control until the early 1920s, when the electorate was asked to choose between political union with South Africa and responsible government. The majority, mostly the poorer white settlers, opted for the latter, and in 1923 Southern Rhodesia became a self-governing colony.

Under the home-rule arrangement the franchise was technically non-racial, but in practice tough property qualifications denied nearly all Africans the vote.

### The middle years

For the next few decades Southern Rhodesia was administered, placidly enough, by settler governments headed by three prime ministers: Sir Charles Coghlan until 1927; H.U. Moffat, grandson of the renowned missionary Robert Moffat, from 1927 until 1933 and thereafter, for 30 years, by the liberal-minded but rather patrician surgeon-politician Godfrey Huggins (later elevated to the peerage as Lord Malvern).

The most significant development on the domestic front during this period was the Land Apportionment Act, a far-reaching piece of legislation passed in 1930. This divided the colony into white areas, 'native reserves' and 'native purchase areas'. Africans could no longer buy land freely (which, in practice, few had been able to do under the old laws), but could do so in the last-mentioned category. The 'white areas' encompassed the towns, where African workers were classed as migrant labour, with 'temporary' status.

These arrangements had more than a passing resemblance to the nascent apartheid system being established south of the Limpopo. Nevertheless they received the approval of missionaries, white liberals, humanitarians and the British Labour government – on the rather negative premise that they would prevent further expropriation, and exploitation of the African, by the expanding settler community.

Southern Rhodesians of all races fought with honour and occasionally with distinction in both world wars. For the country, though, the conflicts held more than military significance: each, and especially the second (1939-45) stimulated industrial and agricultural development, which, in turn, had profound political relevance – economic progress tended to undermine the colonial government's faith in its 'two-pyramid', or separate development, policy; it also provided fresh impetus for emergent African nationalism (see page 27).

### The ill-fated federation

The Afrikaner Nationalist victory at the South African polls in 1948 provoked something of a backlash among English-speaking communities, prompting the British and Southern Rhodesian governments to seek a new territorial dispensation in Central Africa, one that was economically viable enough, on the one hand, to withstand the winds of reaction and race prejudice blowing from the south and, on the other, to resist radical African nationalism at home.

Specifically, it was proposed that Southern Rhodesia and the British protectorates of Northern Rhodesia and Nyasaland come together within a federal arrangement.

After protracted negotiations among the parties involved – Whitehall and the white leadership in Central Africa – the issue was put to Southern Rhodesian voters and, on 1 October 1953, the Federation of the Rhodesias and Nyasaland came into being.

Godfrey Huggins was sworn in as the first federal prime minister (Sir Roy Welensky took over the reins three years later), to be replaced as Southern Rhodesian premier by R.S. Garfield Todd, a moderate social reformist.

The white establishment – the politicians and industrialists – had pushed for amalgamation for both economic and political reasons. The federation, they argued, would bring together Northern Rhodesia's vast copper mines, Nyasaland's pool of cheap labour and Southern Rhodesia's industrial sophistication and access to capital, and the wealth so created would, they believed, enable them among other things to contain militant black nationalism.

The new arrangement was opposed, by both white and black, from the very first. Establishment liberals, among them Todd, took issue with the federal leaders over the pace of African advancement, urging a meaningful degree of political power-sharing and the rapid creation of a prosperous African middle class to act as a buffer against black extremism. In doing so he alienated the majority of Southern Rhodesia's whites, who correctly saw his policies as a threat to their privileged position. In 1958 Todd was replaced by Sir Edgar Whitehead, a somewhat harder-line poliitcian (though still a reformist).

Black nationalists rejected the entire federal structure, had always done so, as an elaborate ploy to delay majority rule.

In 1963, almost exactly a decade after its inception, the federation was dissolved. In the following year Northern Rhodesia and Nyasaland, countries that had been controlled largely from London, were granted their full independence to become, respectively, Zambia and Malawi.

Britain, however, refused to concede Southern Rhodesia the same right until its black and white people reached a mutually acceptable accommodation.

### Black opposition, white reaction

Organized African political opposition began in earnest only in the late 1950s, although small, elite bodies such as the Rhodesia Bantu Voters' Association and the Southern Rhodesian African National Congress (SRANC) lobbied peacefully, and ineffectually – on questions of the vote, land, education, the all-pervading colour bar and so on – well before the Second World War.

The immediate post-war years saw the first successful black industrial actions, among them a general strike (in 1948), and the brief re-emergence of the SRANC. Later, in the mid-1950s, leadership of the opposition movement, now called simply the African National Congress, consolidated under the leadership of Joshua Nkomo, one-time head of the railway workers' union and of the All-Africa Convention (1952).

Banned by Sir Edgar Whitehead in 1959, the ANC was reconstituted as the National Democratic Party (NDP), was again proscribed and immediately resurrected as the Zimbabwe African People's Union (ZAPU). The first politically sponsored guerilla incursions and acts of sabotage began, in a small way, in the early 1960s.

Meanwhile Whitehead, under pressure to increase the pace of reform from both the nationalists and from liberals at home and abroad, produced a new constitution that aimed, vaguely, at political parity between African and settler and, even more vaguely, at eventual majority rule.

The apparently progressive 1961 constitution, and Whitehead's promise to repeal the Land Aportionment Act and to outlaw race discrimination, alienated large sections of the white electorate, and in 1962 the ultra-conservative Rhodesian Front (RF) party, led by Winston Field, was voted into office. It came to power on the white electorate's understanding that it would reverse the reformist trend and – most important – obtain independence from Britain, by agreement if possible but unilaterally if necessary.

Field failed in the latter objective and, in 1964, was replaced by a younger and tougher man: Ian Douglas Smith, a farmer and one-time Royal Air Force fighter pilot now dedicated to the cause of white supremacy.

During this period ZAPU continued to operate externally (and internally, in rather low-key style, as the People's Caretaker Council), though many of its younger, more radical elements were becoming profoundly dissatisfied with the lack of progress towards a democratic dispensation. Led by the Rev. Ndabaningi Sithole, these dissidents broke away in August 1963 to form the Zimbabwe African National Union (ZANU). In the following two years the nationalist movement found itself severely weakened by inter-party violence, and African opposition to the new hard-line regime was effectively stifled by the wholesale imprisonment, detention and restriction of its internal leadership.

On 11 November 1965 Smith, who had refused to accept Britain's minimum conditions for a peaceful transition to independence, unilaterally declared the sovereignty of white-ruled Rhodesia. The act of seizure became known as UDI.

### The years of rebellion

The rebel regime found itself beleaguered from the outset. Not a single country recognized UDI; Harold Wilson's Labour government declared the act illegal and immediately imposed economic sanctions on the colony. The United Nations applied mandatory embargoes in 1968.

By and large, though, the trade restrictions proved ineffective: many western businessmen sidestepped them; South Africa

ABOVE: *Rhodesian premier Ian Smith, flanked by his ministers, signs the rebel 'independence' declaration.*

ignored them; neighbouring African states were forced by economic necessity to deal with and through Rhodesia.

Nevertheless the pressures were mounting and both Wilson and Smith, each for his own reasons, badly needed a settlement. Two abortive attempts at negotiating an end to the conflict were undertaken, both aboard Royal Navy warships (HMS Tiger in 1966; HMS Fearless in 1968) before what appeared to be fruitful talks took place, in 1971, between Smith and the new British premier and leader of the Conservative Party, the aristocratic Sir Alec Douglas-Home.

The Smith-Home agreement contained a number of proposals that would have led to majority rule – at some distant time in the future. It also stipulated that the scheme be 'acceptable to the people as a whole', a condition with which neither government expected any difficulty since, after all, most of the recognized nationalist leaders were either in prison or in exile. A commission, led by British peer Lord Pearce, was dispatched to Rhodesia to test African opinion.

In the event, the proposals were roundly rejected by the great majority. The ordinary Zimbabwean, rural as well as urban, turned out to be a lot more politically sophisticated than the experts had believed. Moreover, opposition to the proposals had been well orchestrated by the African National Council, an ad hoc organization hurriedly put together under the leadership of Bishop Abel Muzorewa, a newcomer to the political arena.

Soon afterwards the internal security situation began to deteriorate sharply. Both ZAPU and ZANU had espoused the armed stuggle in 1966, but guerilla operations, mounted mainly by Nkomo's ZIPRA (ZAPU's military wing) had been conducted at a low level. Now, with the failure of the Pearce exercise, the mobilization of African opinion within Rhodesia and the impending

ABOVE: *Robert Mugabe and Joshua Nkomo pictured after signing the unity agreement in December 1987.*

liberation, by Frelimo forces, of neighbouring Mozambique, the time seemed opportune for a fresh onslaught. In the latter part of 1972 the external division of ZANU (its military wing was known as ZANLA) and soon to be led by Robert Mugabe, opened up a new offensive in the northeast.

### Towards independence

During the mid-1970s, following the liberation of Angola and Mozambique, the United States re-evaluated its Central African policy and began pushing hard for a settlement of the Rhodesian question. So, too, did neighbouring South Africa now intent on 'stabilizing' the region.

Attempts were made at an internal accord: Smith held talks with Muzorewa, leader of the renamed United African National Council (UANC) and with Nkomo. Both exercises initially held promise, but proved abortive.

Robert Mugabe was released from prison, rejoined the guerilla forces in Mozambique and replaced Sithole as leader of ZANU.

In 1976 Smith, pressured by American secretary of state Henry Kissinger, agreed to majority rule 'within two years' (a far cry from his previously stated 'not in my lifetime') and the nationalists were persuaded to attend a British-chaired conference in Geneva. In order to present a unified case the two major political movements, Nkomo's ZAPU and Mugabe's ZANU, joined together in the Patriotic Front (PF).

The 1977 Geneva deliberations came to nothing, however – the Anglo-American proposals, though they contained much of merit, including massive and much-needed international investment in a post-UDI Zimbabwe, were unacceptable to both the Rhodesian Front and the PF, and it wasn't until the following

year that Smith reached an accord with Muzorewa's UANC and the Sithole (minority) faction of ZANU. This made provision for a transitional government to hold the fort until 31 December 1978, after which a new constitution (still favourable to whites) would be implemented.

But the civil conflict intensified, and although in due course Muzorewa did assume office, as premier of Zimbabwe-Rhodesia, his regime failed to win grassroots support. Neither did it gain international respectability: there was widespread belief that the elections that had brought it to power had been rigged, and Muzorewa's dealings with the South African government were suspect. The Patriotic Front continued to wage war.

### The last mile

In August 1979 the leaders of the Commonwealth, meeting in the Zambian capital of Lusaka, called for new all-party talks to bring about a final solution of the Rhodesian impasse. British prime minister Margaret Thatcher prevailed upon the Zambians and Tanzanians to persuade Nkomo and Mugabe – who had created a joint military command but otherwise continued to lead separate organizations – to attend the conference, scheduled to be held at London's Lancaster House under the chairmanship of Lord Carrington, in September. After some hesitation, both agreed to do so.

The principal parties to the talks – Rhodesian Front, ZANU and ZAPU – were in the mood for compromise. And the British government, unlike its predecessors, gave priority to the inclusion (as opposed to the isolation) of the Patriotic Front in the negotiation process.

After 14 weeks of tough bargaining, agreement was finally reached on 21 December 1979. The formula called for a staged progression: first a ceasefire, then a laying down of arms, followed by free and fair (and Commonwealth-supervised) elections, the formation of a new government and, at last, the formal granting of independence.

Despite the difficulties – and there were many – the elections were sucessfully held in February 1980.

ZANU-PF, which had borne the brunt of the fighting during the protracted and bloody bush war, decided to break its association with ZAPU and fight the election on its own platform. Many considered this a tactical mistake at the time. ZANU-PF's leader, Robert Mugabe, despite his record as a founder of the original party in 1963 and 10-year sojourn in Smith's prisons, was generally considered the underdog – Nkomo, it was thought, had greater historical claims to leaderhip of the nationalist movement. Nkomo campaigned under the PF banner.

The electoral outcome took politicians, press and most of the 'informed' public by surprise: ZANU-PF gained no less than 57 of the 80 'African' (common-roll) seats., Nkomo's PF a mere 20, most of them in Matabeleland. Muzorewa's UANC, with just three seats, was annihilated as an effective political force. Predictably, Smith's Rhodesian Front secured all 20 of the seats reserved for whites.

Armed with this massive endorsement, Robert Mugabe formed free Zimbabwe's first government, stressing, in his inaugural address, the need for forgiveness, reconciliation, and reconstruction.

# GOVERNMENT

The Lancaster House Agreement of 1980 made provision for a Westminster-type constitution comprising a bicameral legislature upper and lower, a multi-party 'winner-take-all' electoral system, an executive of prime minister and cabinet and a largely ceremonial state president.

In the interests of a smooth transition of power, however, entrenched clauses guaranteed the white electorate 20 seats in the lower chamber (House of Assembly) and ten seats in the advisory upper house (Senate). The constitution was to remain in force – inviolate – for a period of ten years.

Robert Mugabe and his ZANU-PF party, on the other hand, were firmly committed to creating a Marxist-Leninist social and economic order and, increasingly, to the establishment of a one-party state.

By the mid-1980s support among whites for the old-style Rhodesian Front was in decline. A faction sympathetic to Mugabe had broken away in 1983 to form the Independent Zimbabwe Group, and the RF renamed itself, contesting the 1985 elections as the Conservative Alliance of Zimbabwe (CAZ). At those polls, Mugabe's ZANU-PF increased its parliamentary representation to 64 seats.

Thereafter, Mugabe intensified his efforts towards achieving a de facto one-party state (a de jure one would have to wait until the ten-year moratorium on constitutional change elapsed). Ndabaningi Sithole and Muzorewa had all but been eclipsed, but Nkomo's ZAPU, particularly strong in Matabeleland, remained a powerful minority grouping.

In December 1987, however, following what amounted to a minor civil war in Matabeleland, the two major leaders signed a unity agreement merging their parties under the name of ZANU-PF. Nkomo was appointed one of the two vice-presidents and assumed a senior position in the new cabinet.

At the same time, substantial constitutional changes were being pushed through. The guaranteed white seats were abolished in September 1987, and the remaining members of the lower chamber were asked to elect 20 new members to their assembly and ten to the upper. All the candidates were nominated by ZANU-PF, and the final choice gave whites eleven seats in the Assembly and four in the Senate.

During the following month parliament made further constitutional amendments, converting the ceremonial presidency into an executive office incorporating the post of prime minister. Mugabe, the sole nominee, was installed as Zimbabwe's first executive state president on 31 December 1987. His government included a new 'super cabinet' comprising Joshua Nkomo and three senior ministers.

Two years later the Senate was formally abolished and the remaining chamber enlarged to 150 members, of whom 120 were directly elected, twelve nominated by the president, ten were traditional chiefs and eight were provincial governors. The life of this restructured House of Assembly is six years.

The president also holds office for six years. Candidates must be nominated by no fewer than ten members of the House of Assembly. The president acts on the advice of the cabinet which, in 1990, consisted of 21 ministers, together with seven ministers of state in the president's office. Other features of the constitution include:

*A declaration of rights*, which guarantees the basic human rights and freedoms regardless of race, place of origin, political opinion, colour, creed or sex.

*An ombudsman*, appointed by the president to investigate complaints against officials of central and local government.

*A chief's council*, chosen by chiefs appointed by the president.

The drive towards a one-party state seems to have been suspended, if not abandoned, as have moves to create a socialist order based on Marxist-Leninist principles: with the collapse of the Soviet empire in the late 1980s and early 1990s, and the global trend towards fully democratic institutions and market economies, both objectives have been running counter to the mood of the times.

Indeed, strong opposition to a unitary political system has been expressed both in the country at large and within the ranks of the ruling party, and in August 1990 the ZANU-PF politburo voted to reject plans for a one-party state.

## The law

The Zimbabwean constitution is the country's highest judicial authority. The legal system is Roman-Dutch, a code based on that of the Cape of Good Hope, which originated in turn from the Germanic laws of western Europe, many of which were derived from four great books prescribed by the sixth-century Eastern Roman emperor Justinian.

Overlaying the Zimbabwean code, and modifying it, is the body of statute law – parliamentary legislation.

The Supreme Court acts as a court of appeal on all matters except those touching on fundamental rights, in which it has original jurisdiction. The court comprises the chief justice and four judges of appeal.

Other judicial bodies, in order of precedence, are the High Court, consisting of the Chief Justice and eleven other judges; the regional courts, which have criminal jurisdiction, and the magistrates' courts, which deal with civil as well as lesser criminal matters. The traditional customary-law and primary courts, which function mainly in the rural areas, have now been incorporated into the formal legal system. They comprise about a thousand village and about a hundred community tribunals. During the years since the advent of the new order the judiciary has retained its independence, firmly discounting political pressures, and is widely regarded for its uncompromising integrity.

## Defence

Integration of the three large, undefeated and hostile armed forces – those of the Rhodesian government, ZANLA and ZIPRA – at independence in 1980 proceeded, contrary to widely expressed fears, with remarkable smoothness. Zimbabwe now has a standing army of 53 000, including the much-publicized North Korean-trained 5th Brigade, and a small air force complement of 2 500.

There is also a subtstantial people's militia, and a police force of around 15 000.

Among the main preoccupations of the defence establishment have been the threat of military strikes by a South Africa intent on destabilizing the region, and the Zimbabwean commitment to aid the Mozambican government in its struggle against the Renamo (also known as MNR) dissidents.

Since President De Klerk's succession to office and the subsequent release of Nelson Mandela in February 1990, the danger of armed incursion from the south has receded dramatically. At the time of writing, though, some 10 000 Zimbabwean troops were still deployed in Mozambique, most of them along the economically vital Mutare-Beira transport corridor, and sporadic skirmishing had been a feature of the common border area in the east. However, progress towards a peaceful conclusion to Mozambique's civil war was gaining momentum.

## Foreign policy

Zimbabwe belongs in the non-aligned group of nations, though the classification began to lose much of its meaning with the ending of the cold war, and to an informal, historically anti-South African grouping known as the 'frontline states'.

The country has played a leading role in the Southern African Development Co-ordination Conference (SADCC), an association of states established to lessen dependence on South Africa. The latter country, though, is a regional superpower and Zimbabwe must of necessity conduct much of its trade with, and use the sophisticated road and rail systems of, its large and economically advanced southern neighbour.

For these reasons, and for fear of reprisals, Mugabe denied the South African liberation groups bases from which to conduct the armed struggle of the 1980s. He did, however, extend political and diplomatic support to movements endorsed by the Organisation of African Unity (OAU). Similarly, he supported the principle of economic sanctions but admitted that Zimbabwe could not, herself, afford to apply comprehensive trade and financial embargoes.

Relations between the two countries began to improve significantly after South African leaders began negotiating a fully democratic dispensation in the early 1990s. Sporting links were re-established following South Africa's readmittance to the international cricket arena in the latter half of 1991. More significant, a Zimbabwean cabinet minister met with his South African counterpart, in Cape Town, in April 1992 to agree a common strategy for regional famine relief.

## Health and education

Most Zimbabweans live in the rural areas, many of which suffer from periodic drought, some of them from 'desertification'. Medical and health facilities, though improving, generally remain below First World standards; malnutrition is widespread in years of poor rainfall; malaria is a growing problem, as is Aids; measles and pneumonia are major causes of death.

Nevertheless much is being done, through the hospitals and rural health centres, in the realms of mother-and-child care, nutrition, disease control, environmental hygiene and immunization, and Aids prevention. Across the board, the country has one physician for every 7 000 persons, and one hospital bed among 450.

Among social services provided by the government are child welfare, old-age benefits and care of the aged, and a degree of public assistance.

Huge strides have been made in the field of mass-education since independence in 1980. Primary schooling (ages 7-14) is free and compulsory for all; between 1979 and 1987 the total number of primary pupils rose from 820 000 to 2,3 million (92 percent of the total possible). Secondary education, which lasts for six years, is undertaken in the country's 1 500 secondary schools, up from just 177 in 1980.

Altogether a most gratifying record. The spectacular improvements in educational standards, though, were achieved at enormous financial cost and have not been matched by a commensurate increase in employment opportunities, a situation which has created its own, and currently intractable, problems. In the long term, however – once the southern African region stabilizes and there is real economic growth – this investment in Zimbabwe's youth should pay handsome dividends.

# THE ECONOMY

During the 1980s and early 1990s Zimbabwe's economic growth – 3,2 percent a year, which appears fairly healthy at first glance but which barely kept up with population increase – was uneven, plagued by fluctuating world commodity prices, poor rains in many years, and by government policies that have constrained investment.

The ruling party came to power on a fixed Marxist-Leninist platform but has been cautious in its application of socialist principles, and the economy remains what is described as 'semi-developed mixed, with some state participation'. The government has avoided outright nationalization.

Nevertheless, the first decade of independence witnessed a proliferation of parastatal bodies, the creation of a state-run minerals marketing corporation, government-private enterprise joint ventures, 'state capitalism' (the purchase, by government, of equity stakes), and relentless pressure to 'Zimbabweanize' the private sector. During the decade, too, there was an inhibitive increase in bureaucratic red tape and the imposition of far-reaching controls over private businesses – on prices, minimum wages, dismissals, retrenchments, currency exchange and imports, the remittance of dividends, the hiring of expatriates and so forth. In short, Zimbabwe in the 1980s had something approaching a command economy – government controlled 60 percent of exports, 100 percent of imports, owned four of the ten largest companies quoted on the local stock exchange, and employed a quarter of the national workforce.

The effects have, generally, been adverse. Per capita wealth creation has remained static; unemployment had risen to a million before the end of the 1980s (300 000 secondary school leavers come onto the job market each year) and investment, which the country desperately needs, has stagnated.

Still, the economic outlook is far from bleak – provided official intent is translated into decisive action. In 1989 President Robert Mugabe announced a major policy shift towards a fully market-based system which, if followed through, should produce an annual growth rate of between 5 and 6 percent.

A high figure, but attainable: the country has a great deal going for it in terms of natural resources, developed infrastructure, technical expertise and entrepreneurial skills.

## Transport

Zimbabwe has a fine network of roads – 85 800 km of them, of which 14 000 are designated as primary and secondary highways. In the later 1980s registered commercial vehicles numbered 66 000, passenger vehicles 265 000.

The national 3394-km rail system, largely diesel-operated, connects with that of Botswana to the southwest (which in turn is linked to South Africa's railways), with the South African network through Beitbridge, with Zambia over the Victoria Falls bridge, and with Mozambique through Mutare (to Beira) and from a point near Gweru southeast to Maputo. In 1986 the Beira Corridor Group was formed to provide an alternative transport link to the route running through South Africa. During the 1980s the railways carried some 3 million passengers and over 12 million tonnes of freight annually.

Air Zimbabwe operates passenger and cargo services to countries in Africa (including South Africa) and, among other destinations, Britain, Germany, Greece, Cyprus and Australia. Domestic services connect the major Zimbabwean centres. At the end of the 1980s the airline was transporting half a million passengers a year (passenger-kilometres totalled 700 million).

## Energy

Zimbabwe has been obliged to import most of its fuel needs and, during the 1980s, much of its electricity as well. Oil is brought in via the Beira-Mutare pipeline and is processed at the Feruka refinery near the latter city. Mozambican insurgents occasionally disrupted the supplies during the first decade of Zimbabwean independence.

The country's coal reserves are estimated at 28 billion tonnes; its sole producer the Wankie (Hwange) colliery, which ran at well below capacity for much of the 1980s, though its opera-

ABOVE: *Zimbabwe has a highly developed road transport system based on a sound infrastructure.*

tions were expanded at the end of the decade. The colliery produces around 160 000 tonnes of coke a year. The Lubimbi coalfield, with calculated reserves of 20 billion tonnes, is the site of an ambitious oil-from-coal project.

Zimbabwe and Zambia share the giant Kariba hydro-electric facilities, though for decades the only power station was linked to the Zambian side. In the later 1980s Zimbabwe commissioned its own Kafue plant to add 920 MW of new thermal capacity to the national grid, but the installation was seriously damaged by fire in 1989. Kafue was scheduled to come back on stream in the early 1990s, so eliminating the need to import. The disastrous drought of 1992 adversely affected power generation.

To date, the Hwange thermal power station has accounted for just over half the total national generating capacity (1 900 MW). There are longer-term development plans for a 300-MW plant at Kariba and two other hydro-electric installations on the Zambezi River, together involving an investment of around US$4 billion.

## Agriculture

Land redistribution has ranked high among government priorities since the early 1980s – understandably so since, at independence, 4 000 white commercial farmers owned 78 percent of the better land (classified Grades l and ll). Indeed, in the minds of most rural Africans, the war of liberation was as much about land as it was about the vote, and grassroots pressure for reform has been intense.

Again, the authorities proceeded with caution – principally to avoid damaging the confidence of white Zimbabweans generally and the farmers in particular, and that of foreign investors. By the end of the decade just 45 000 rural families had been resettled on three million hectares which had been acquired on a willing-seller, willing-buyer basis. At that time, nearly five million Zimbabweans were living on the lower grades (IV and V) of land and practised subsistence farming methods.

Although white farmers produce about three-quarters of the national commercial crop, and on average four times more per hectare than their peasant counterparts, they do so because their soils are generally far more fertile. When the resources are evenly matched – on Grade II land for example – productivity is almost on a par.

Among other statistics that have come to light: peasant farmers have accounted for fully 80 percent of the increase in the national maize crop since independence, and are responsible for over half the total cotton output. African farmers resettled during the 1980s have also begun to grow tobacco and barley, two of the more 'difficult' crops.

Encouraging trends indeed, brought sharply into focus when Zimbabwe donated 25 000 tonnes of maize to Ethiopian famine relief in 1985 – the first African country to do so.

All this is significant in the context of the government's most recent, and highly controversial, plans to force through the compulsory purchase of around 5 million hectares of the rich and mostly white-owned 'maize and tobacco belt'.

Agriculture contributes between 11 and 17 percent of Zimbabwe's gross domestic product (depending on the kindness or otherwise of the rains: the 1991-2 season was a disaster), and employs 70 percent of the total labour force. Maize is the staple food crop; other cereals include wheat, millet, sorghum and barley; the principal cash crops are tobacco (a leading earner of foreign exchange), cotton and sugar, groundnuts, sunflower seed, tea, coffee, citrus and other fruits.

In 1985 plans were announced for a Z$188 million palm-oil scheme. During the 1980s Zimbabwe was one of only two sub-Saharan countries permitted to export beef to the European (Economic) Community. The national cattle herd totals some 5,5 million head.

TOP: *Farm workers tend tobacco fields near Marondera.*
CENTRE: *Much land is still farmed by traditional methods.*
LEFT: *Some 15 percent of Zimbabwe is classed as rangeland; half the national herd is owned by peasant stock-farmers.*

## Mining

Zimbabwe is blessed with over 40 different exploitable minerals, of which the most significant in value terms are gold, nickel, high-grade chromium, copper, iron, coal and asbestos. Gold accounts for some 35 percent of mineral export earnings.

Mining's contribution to GDP declined from 10 percent in 1980 to 7 percent towards the end of the decade (world commodity prices were unfavourable, and to compound the problem local production and transport costs spiralled) but, still, minerals earn the country about a third of its export revenue. Plans have been announced for.a 3 000-tonne per annum plant to refine copper and manufacture copper products.

## Manufacturing

The country's manufacturing sector is, after South Africa's, the second most sophisticated on the sub-Saharan continent.

Industrial development during the first half of the century was stimulated by energetic mineral exploration and exploitation, proximity to the advanced infrastructure of the country's southern neighbour, demand for raw materials during two world wars, and by the post-war influxes of skilled immigrants. Later, the federal experiment (see page 26) and, most notable, sanctions and the need for import replacement during the years of rebellion, politically disastrous though this period may have been, each provided a powerful economic impetus. There was also consumer-led growth after independence in 1980.

At the end of the decade secondary industry employed close on 160 000 people, contributed 31 percent of GDP, about a third of total export earnings, and growth was running at a respectable 5,6 percent a year. Shortage of foreign exchange, however, has put a brake on further substantial expansion.

The country manufactures a wide variety of goods. Among those that have performed well (in volume terms) in recent times are transport equipment, clothing and footwear, and chemical and petroleum products.

---

The past three decades have been troubled ones for Zimbabwe. The demise of colonialism in Africa, rebellion, civil war and the agonies of transition have taken their toll, and the country is still, in the early 1990s, in the process of painful adjustment to new circumstances, to a new world. That it will emerge with credit, and in prosperity, is more than a possibility – if stability returns to the region as a whole, it is almost a certainty.

Meanwhile, there is much about the country that has been and always will be unaffected by the trauma of change. Zimbabwe's natural treasures are immutable: her scenic splendours, her superb wildlife, the wide and sunny spaces will continue to beckon, whatever the future holds.

BELOW: *Tea estates in the Honde valley in the scenically spectacular eastern region.*

South of Bulawayo, Zimbabwe's second city, lie the massive, jumbled formations of the Matobo hills, once home to the San (or Bushmen) and a place of deep religious significance to the later Karanga. The word Matobo means 'bald heads', and was conferred by the great Ndebele soldier-king Mzilikazi in one of his more whimsical moments: the huge rounded domes and whalebacks of the region reminded him of an assembly of his elders. This spectacular concentration of outcrops, 2 000 km² in extent, is part of an enormously ancient geological system: the rocks are estimated to have been formed 3 000 million years ago, when the planet earth was still young.

**PREVIOUS PAGE:** *Part of the Matobo national park, a 44 000-ha area of rock and msasa woodland set aside for game. The park is renowned for its sizeable leopard population and, especially, for its magnificent array of birds of prey, including large numbers of black eagles.*

**BELOW:** *The beautiful flat lizard, a common denizen of the Matobos. These are sociable creatures, congregating in dense colonies among the sunlit rocks. The various southern African species – 10 in all – are most easily identified by the coloration of the brightly-hued males.*

**ABOVE:** *On the summit of World's View in the Matobo hills is the grave of Cecil John Rhodes, the 'immense and brooding spirit' who, in 1890, sent his Pioneer Column into Mashonaland to inaugurate nine decades of British colonial rule. Three years later the settlers invaded and occupied Matebeleland. Rhodes died in Cape Town, South Africa, in 1902 and his body, in accordance with his last wishes, was carried 2 000 km northwards, across the Limpopo River, to be buried in the place he had loved best.*

RIGHT: *The rock elephant shrew (Elephantulus myurus), so named for its elongated, flexible snout. This insectivore, a familiar sight in the Matobos, tends to be a solitary little animal, invariably found sheltering in the shade of a convenient boulder or rocky overhang during the hotter daylight hours.*

**ABOVE:** *The Matobo hills are famed for the bizarre shapes of their rocky outcrops, natural structures created during the cooling of the earth's surface three billion years ago and refined over succeeding aeons by the action of wind and water. This column comprises two perfectly balanced blocks of granite.*

**LEFT:** *Well-maintained roads provide visitors with comfortable access to the Matobo national park, a place of craggy, hauntingly beautiful landscapes, of far horizons, profound silence and a pervasive air of primeval mystery. The magnificent black eagle (Aquila verreauxi), a much persecuted but – happily – still fairly common bird of prey, makes its home among the high cliffs and outcrops, feeding on the dassies, or rock-rabbits, that abound and on guineafowl, young antelope and young baboon. It will also prey on the larger buck species.*

39

OPPOSITE PAGE: *The Kame complex of stone-walled structures, 16 km from Bulawayo, was among the last and most impressive settlements built by the ancient Rosvi people and is now one of Zimbabwe's four World Heritage Sites. The great walled terraces, many of them patterned, were constructed during the 15th and 16th centuries, the Rosvi communities flourishing until Mzilikazi's invading Ndebele occupied the land at the end of the 1830s. For decades thereafter Kame was held as 'the king's preserve' - hallowed ground, venue for sacred ceremonies and a secret place hidden from inquisitive European eyes until 1893, when Lobengula, the last Ndebele ruler, fled from the advancing settler columns to die in the wilderness. The first formal investigation of the site, by the Rhodesia Ancient Ruins Company, was faulty in its conception, destructive in its execution, and much of the priceless legacy was lost for ever.*

RIGHT: *One of the Matobo's many strange balancing-rock formations.*

BELOW, LEFT: *This fine example of San (Bushman) art can be seen in the Nswatugi cave, deep within the Matobo hills. The region boasts nearly a hundred decorated shelters and many more 'canvases' of exposed granite. The paintings date to the Late Stone Age (few of them are in fact older than 2 000 years) and are similar in style to those of the Natal Drakensberg. The colours these ancient master-artists used were derived from the mineral oxides of the earth: manganese to produce black, zinc to produce white, and iron the deep browns, reds and yellows.*

BELOW, RIGHT: *A klipspringer (Oreotragus oreotragus) in one of the more densely wooded parts of the Matobo national park. These antelope are especially well adapted to rugged, rocky terrain. They are able to go without water for long periods.*

Bulawayo's tree-garlanded thorough-fares are unusually wide: they were originally designed, in the 1890s, to allow eight-span oxwagons to manoeuvre with ease. It was declared a town in 1894, and elevated to municipal status three years later, when the railway line from Vryburg, in South Africa's north-eastern Cape Province, was completed. Today the city, capital of the Matabeleland region, is a flourishing communications and industrial centre (textiles, tyre manufacturing, vehicles, electronic goods, food-processing, printing and packaging) of some half-million citizens, most of them of Ndebele stock.

OPPOSITE PAGE: *Flamboyants, or royal poincianas, grace the approaches to the colonial-style main post office building.*

BELOW: *An attractive open-air display of local crafts. Street vendors make up a large part of the expanding 'informal economy'.*

RIGHT: *Outside the Bulwayo Club, for decades the exclusive haunt of the city's business community.*

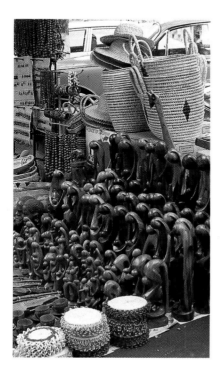

Bulawayo is the centre of the national rail system, and visitors can spend an intriguing few hours at the city's railways museum. The 2 745-km network is largely diesel-operated, but some steam locomotives, including these grand old workhorses at the marshalling yards, are still performing with honour. Most of the early locomotives were small tankers (they had an average traction power of less than 90 kilonewtons), operated by saturated steam, and had side valves. Later, in 1911, came the super-heating of steam, followed by various other improvements, including the automatic bypass valve, mechanical stokers and lubrication, roller-bearing axle boxes and, in the late 1920s, the articulated locomotive. Pictured above left is an old Class 12; above, Class 14 and left, a Class 16.

**OPPOSITE PAGE:** Some of the engine fitters who keep the old steam driven locos on track.

46

RIGHT AND OPPOSITE: *Bulawayo is a place of flowering trees – lilac jacarandas in springtime, bauhinias and, perhaps most striking of all, the blood-red royal poincianas of summer. The latter – which, oddly enough, belongs to the pea family – is better known as the flamboyant (Delonix regia), a native of Madagascar. The city tends to look parched for much of the year – this is a low-rainfall region, and drought has been a grimly persistent reality during the past decade (there are imaginative proposals to bring the waters of the Zambezi, 400 km away, to the region) - but for all that the suburban gardens remain colourful and gloriously green throughout the seasons.*

ABOVE: *The Bulawayo region, and especially the ruggedly splendid Matobo hills to the south, is renowned for its birds of prey; one of the more common is the striking bateleur (Terathopius ecaudatus).*
RIGHT: *One of the Bulawayo area's prime tourist attractions is the Chipangali wildlife orphanage, a research centre and sanctuary for sick and injured animals, some of which are returned to the wild on recovery. Inmates range from massively bulky rhino down to the smallest of mammals. Here, one of the orphanage's assistants comforts an infant baboon.*

**RIGHT:** *Cattle cluster in the dry Bembesi river-bed in the Lupane district of northern Matabeleland. Most of the region is occupied by peasant stock-farmers; altogether, about a seventh of Zimbabwe is classed as rangeland, and half the national herd belongs to communities practising traditional pasturalism. Zimbabwean beef is known for its excellence.*

**BELOW:** *One of the oddities of the Zimbabwean veld is the dung-beetle (family Scarabaeidae), whose diet consists solely of animal droppings. The beetle scoops and rakes these into a ball that is often much larger than its own body (it is sometimes assisted in this by another beetle – not necessarily its mate, but rather a self-invited guest) and then rolls it away to bury it a few centimetres below the ground. The female scarab will create an underground chamber for the ball, and divide the dung into pear-shaped lumps on which she lays her eggs.*

Zimbabwe's premier game sanctuary is the Hwange national park, a vast (15 000-km²), flattish, heat-hazed expanse of Kalahari sandveld, grassy plain, bush thicket and mopane woodland that is believed to contain the widest variety and densest concentration of wildlife in the world. Here there are no perennial streams or rivers, but the animals are sustained by the many natural pans of the region and, in the dry winter months, by man-made waterholes.

FAR LEFT: *Elephant make their way to the inviting waters of Caterpillar pan. The picture was taken in the dry season, when upwards of 20 000 of these gentle giants make their home in the park. When the summer rains come, in November and December, many of the herds disperse, some trekking as far afield as the Okavango delta in northern Botswana.*

ABOVE LEFT: *The entrance to Hwange's Main camp, 17 km beyond the Gwai River and 265 km from Bulwayo on the road to Victoria Falls. Main camp offers comfortable lodges, chalets and two-bedroomed cottages, guided walks, restaurant, bar and grocery shop.*

BELOW LEFT: *This male red-headed weaver (Anaplectes rubriceps) is busy building its neat, remarkably tough nest. The female lays her eggs – usually a clutch of three, and greenish-blue in colour – between October and December.*

FOLLOWING PAGES: *A group of impala (Aepyceros melampus) make their way to Big Tom's waterhole. These reddish-brown antelope, found in great numbers in the savanna regions of southern Africa, are renowned for their prodigious leaps (over 3 m in height) when alarmed. A herd in flight moves across the veld in gracefully synchro-nized, almost ballet-like fashion, hundreds of individuals veering and bounding in precise unison.*

OPPOSITE PAGE: *The king at rest. Hwange is home to 25 predator species, most formidable of which is the lion. This is Africa's largest carnivore, an animal that hunts and kills by a subtly complex process – one in which the female usually plays the dominant role. The male tends to be less active but, when moved to do so, is able to show a quite remarkable turn of speed, covering 100 m in just four to six seconds. Lion can be found in prides of up to 30, but family units usually number five or six individuals.*

LEFT: *A solitary roan antelope (Hippotragus equinus) in its lightly wooded habitat. The roan, a relatively rare bovid species, is distinguished by the black and white markings of its face and its heavily ringed, backward-curving horns. The species is found mainly in eastern Zimbabwe, northern Botswana and on the plains of eastern Transvaal.*

RIGHT: *More than 400 species of bird can be observed in the Hwange park in the summer months, including the three-streaked tchagra (Tchagra australis), a member of the shrike family. This bird has a distinctive flight-song during the breeding season (October to January): a descending series of whistles uttered as it spirals down from the high treetops. It feeds exclusively on insects, which it pursues on the ground or gleans from low bushes.*

LEFT: *Hwange has three major camps and a number of smaller ones, including the exclusive Deka, Lukosi and Bumbusi clusters of cottages, chalets and lodges – restful oases in an otherwise magnificently pristine wilderness, each linked to the others and with the great open spaces by a 480-km network of mostly gravelled game-viewing roads. Main camp has an airstrip; just beyond the park's boundaries are five hotels and a number of less formal venues, among them the luxurious Hwange Safari and Ivory lodges. The picture shows attractive tree-house accommodation at Ivory Lodge.*

BELOW: *Elephant huddle companionably at the Dopi pan. While the northern segment of the park has been fairly extensively developed for tourism, the vast southern areas remain an untouched wilderness. Game-viewing is especially rewarding during the dry winter months, when the vegetation has thinned out and the animals congregate at the waterholes in their thousands.*

**ABOVE LEFT:** *A juvenile spotted hyaena (Crocuta crocuta) stays close to its mother in the lushness of Hwange's summer grasslands. The species, much commoner than its brown cousin (Hyaena brunnea), has immensely strong jaws that enable it to crunch the bones of carrion, but contrary to popular belief it is an accomplished hunter as well as a scavenger, capable of catching and bringing down full-grown antelope. The hyaena's sinister reputation (a quite undeserved one) derives partly from its repertoire of eerie 'laughs', 'chuckles' and 'giggles'.*
**ABOVE:** *The colourful ground hornbill (Bucorvus leadbeateri) is a large and mostly terrestrial bird that feeds in the veld on insects, frogs, lizards and rodents. Its distinctive call, a loudly booming sound, often heralds the dawn.*

RIGHT: *The glory, and the infinite peace, of the Hwange veld at sunset. This is the Mataka waterhole in the Dete Vlei area just beyond the Park's north-eastern boundary.*
ABOVE: *Giving way to heavy traffic approaching from the left.*
LEFT: *The pearl-spotted owl (Glaucidium perlatum) is a widely distributed African bird of prey and a common resident of Hwange. The smallest of the owl family (just 19 cm in body length) in the region, it is easily identified by its lack of ears and by the pearly spots on its back and tail. Though generally nocturnal, it can sometimes be observed flying around during the daylight hours.*
OVERLEAF: *A herd of buffalo (Syncerus caffer) in a clearing surrounded by the autumnal colours of mopane bush on the northern plains of the Hwange park. These massive relatives of the antelope are sociable, shy creatures but, when wounded, rank among the most dangerous of Africa's game animals. Their principal natural enemy is the African lion.*

LEFT: *Great numbers of Burchell's zebra (Equus burchellii) can be seen on the plains of Hwange, often in the company of blue wildebeest and other antelope, who draw close to take advantage of the zebra's alertness and superb eyesight. These horse-like animals live in small family groups comprising a single stallion and several mares with their foals, though when the rains have been generous and the grazing is good the families will mingle in much larger groups.*

RIGHT: *The graceful southern reedbuck (Redunca arundinium), a medium-sized antelope that runs with a curious rocking gait, its brown tail held high to show the white underside. Only the rams have horns, which are forward-curving.*

ABOVE: *Leopards are fairly common in Hwange's northern areas, where there are mopane and teak forests and scatters of rocky outcrops. The species (Panthera pardus) is solitary and hunts mostly at night, preying on the smaller buck, on baboons, rock-rabbits (dassies) and even, occasionally, on birds. It is an agile climber, perfectly at ease in the high branches of a tree, and will often use the fork of the trunk as a 'larder' in which to cache the uneaten remains of a kill, often an animal larger than itself. During the daylight hours it tends to lie up, but remains an elusive animal, difficult for visitors to spot: the pattern of black rosettes on its tawny-yellow body enables it to blend beautifully with its surroundings.*

**ABOVE:** *The attractive viewing hide at Big Tom's waterhole.*
**LEFT:** *The delicate gifbol or red posy (Boophane disticha), one of Hwange's many species of bulbous plants, in its early springtime glory. After the fruit ripens, the elongated flower-stalks die and break from the bulb to roll away in the light breeze, distributing its seeds on the journey. At odds with its lovely appearance, though, is the deadly poison the plant contains – a toxin known to the San (Bushman) hunters and used on their arrows.*

**OPPOSITE PAGE:** *Elephant at Big Tom's waterhole, one of Hwange's most rewarding game-viewing spots. These gentle giants have no enemies except man – but, in Africa, that is enemy enough. Poaching has been a serious problem throughout the sub-Saharan part of the continent in recent years; some of the elephant populations have been devastated to the point of regional extinction. Zimbabwe, though, has earned itself an honourable place in the annals of conservation, and the herds have remained healthy and large.*

The Victoria Falls, known as
Mosi-oa-Tunya – the 'smoke that
thunders' – are almost twice as wide
and twice as deep as their Niagara
cousins, spanning the entire 1 700-m
breadth of the Zambezi River to
plunge 108 sheer metres to the gorge
below in a series of magnificent
cataracts. During the peak April
period the waters flow at the rate of
620 000 kilolitres a minute, which
is enough to supply four times
Johannesburg's yearly needs.
ABOVE: An attractively patterned
acraea butterfly.
OPPOSITE: The rim, or lip, of
the huge Zambezi gorge at Victoria
Falls is sliced into a number of seg-
ments by promontories, depressions
and islands, dividing the river's flow
into separate falls and cataracts –
Eastern, Rainbow, Horseshoe, Main
and Devil's. The waters are caught
up in the deep, narrow chasm
between the falls and the opposite,
parallel wall, on the summit of
which is the enchanting woodland
area known as the Rain Forest.

OPPOSITE PAGE: *The Eastern Cataract, seen on the right of the picture, shows a face that is bare during the period of low flow. At peak flood, though, it presents an entirely different aspect, the waters plunging over the lip in a thunderously spectacular torrent. Along one stretch – opposite the Rainbow Falls – the entire volume of the Zambezi roars through a narrow chasm, at the end of which is a deep pool known as the Boiling Pot.*

RIGHT: *The great missionary and explorer David Livingstone surveys a scene 'which must have been gazed upon by angels in their flight'. Livingstone reached the falls by dugout canoe, catching his first full glimpse of their magnificence – from a spray-clouded island on the rim – on 17 November 1855. On the following day he planted the seeds of apricot, peach and coffee, and carved his name on a tree – the only time in his life, he recalled, that he had 'indulged in this weakness'. He was to visit the falls on two more occasions.*

RIGHT AND FAR RIGHT: *Among the many flowering plants that flourish around the falls and its forest are the delicate wild violet (Monopsis decipiens) and the blood-red snake lily (Scadoxus multiflorus spp multi-florus), a member of the cosmopolitan Amarayllidaceae family.*

*Brilliantly bizarre costume, music, folklore, comedy and vibrant dance evoke the spirit of ancient cultures at the Falls Craft Village. All of Zimbabwe's major groupings are represented, including the Shangaan of the east (left) and the Makishi (below), in this 'living museum', which also features traditional homes, arts and crafts and other components of a lifestyle that is fast succumbing to western influences. The Shangaan are an offshoot of the eastern Nguni (Zulu) people. Another prominent dance group is the Nyau, of Malawian and Zambian origin.*

**ABOVE:** *A wood-carver puts the finishing touches to his newest creation at the Falls Craft Village. Much of the work on display is in the category of 'airport art', but some of it has real artistic merit.*

**RIGHT:** *A kaleidoscope of soapstone and hardwood carvings for the passing tourist trade.*

**OPPOSITE PAGE:** *The falls are at their most dramatic in the months following the rainy season – between February and May. During the period of lowest flow, from September to November, most of the water finds its way through and over the Devil's Cataract, leaving three of the other 'falls' - Eastern, Armchair and Rainbow – virtually dry. Even at these times, though, they have their own, special beauty.*

LEFT: *The distinctive silhouette of the fruit-eating trumpeter hornbill (Bycanistes bucinator) at rest in the Rain Forest, a moist and magically misty patch of woodland overlooking the Zambezi gorge at Victoria Falls. These hornbills are found as far north as Kenya, most commonly in large trees along the banks of rivers, though they do make forays into drier, more open country in search of food. They are a sociable species, flocking together in small groups that are often mobbed by smaller birds. Among other residents of the Rain Forest are the blue waxbill, the tchagra, the prinia, black-eyed bulbuls, sunbirds, firefinches, Heuglin's robin and the paradise flycatcher.*

TOP LEFT: *Phoenix reclinata palms of the Victoria Falls forest. This cluster-palm, which is especially prolific in the Natal coastal belt of South Africa's eastern seaboard, derives its common name from the way its stems lean out from the centre. Also known as the wild date (its fruit is edible), it is one of seven species of palm, falling into five genera, that are indigenous to southern Africa.*

OPPOSITE PAGE: *The Devil's Cataract, an impressive and very beautiful sight even during times of low flow. On a clear day the cloud of spray that rises can be seen 70 km away.*

RIGHT AND ABOVE: *White-water rafting and canoeing are some of the more adventurous ways of exploring the mighty Zambezi River. The sport, though, is a lot less dangerous than it looks: there are thrills aplenty, but very few spills. The river rises in the Lunda uplands of Zambia, far to the north, and runs south and then east to form the Zambia-Zimbabwe border before entering Mozambique to discharge into the Indian Ocean a full 3 540 km from its source. It is Africa's fourth largest river – and the least spoilt.*

OPPOSITE PAGE: *A shy bushbuck ewe (Tragelaphus scriptus) shelters in the deep-green depths of the Rain Forest, part of the 2 340-ha Victoria Falls national park and an area rich in animal and plant life. The bushbuck, an antelope related to the kudu, is common throughout the wooded regions of sub-Saharan Africa. The one pictured here is a Chobe bushbuck, a member of the ornatus subspecies.*

LEFT ABOVE: *The endearing paradise flycatcher (Terpsiphone viridis), a species easily identified by it long russet tail-feathers. The bird makes its home in riverine woodlands from South Africa to Cameroon and Ethiopia, nesting in the forks or cross-branches of trees (its nest is a neat affair of fine roots, bark and fibre disguised by an overlay of lichens). The clutch usually comprises three cream-coloured eggs tinged with chestnut-red spots.*

LEFT CENTRE: *Vervet monkey (Cercopithecus aethiops) and infant, one of only three southern African species of this large primate family; the others are the shy samango monkey (C. mitis) of the riverine forests and the chacma baboon (Papio ursinus). Vervets are sociable little creatures, friendly to non-threatening humans (they tend to congregate around game-park camps and other outdoor tourism venues) and are invariably seen in troops of 20 and more.*

LEFT BELOW: *The strikingly handsome narina trogon (Apaloderma narina), a common, yet furtive, forest bird that feeds on insects and caterpillars. The species was named by the celebrated 18th-century naturalist and traveller Francois le Valliant in honour of a beautiful Khoikhoi girl called Narina.*

*The United Touring Company's launch Lukhulu on its sunset trip on the still waters of the Zambezi above the Victoria Falls. Excursions are both fascinating and convivial; passengers enjoy sundowners as they are introduced to the magic and the mysteries of one of Africa's greatest watercourses. Other visitors explore the area by light aircraft, and on foot along pathways and guided walks. The more intrepid negotiate the waters (below the falls) by raft. Ashore, in and around Victoria Falls township, there are sophisticated hotels, casinos, restaurants, supermarket, craft village, crocodile ranch, golf course and the many attractions of the Victoria Falls and Zambezi national parks. The Victoria Falls Hotel, most venerable of the buildings, dates from 1905, the year the renowned railway bridge spanning the river was completed (it was later enlarged to accommodate vehicle and pedestrian traffic).*

OPPOSITE PAGE ABOVE, AND BELOW:
*The broad and deceptively placid-looking reaches of the Zambezi above the falls. The river does not gather speed as it approaches the gorge: the first signs of the impending downrush is a tumultuous roar and, often, the veil of spray that rises fully 300 m into the air.*

OPPOSITE PAGE BELOW: *The commercial ranch at Victoria Falls encloses some 2 000 specimens of the Nile crocodile (Crocodylus niloticus), giant reptiles that are found in rivers from northern Natal and the Transvaal lowveld to Botswana and Zimbabwe. In its natural habitat it feeds on a variety of fish and animals, killing its larger prey by submerging and drowning it. Much of its day is spent basking in the life-giving heat of the sun.*

LEFT: *The impala lily, or Sabi star (Adenium multiflorum), is a familiar sight in the Zambezi valley. A protected species in Zimbabwe, its clusters of star-shaped flowers appear in winter and early spring.*

OPPOSITE PAGE: *The quiet splendour of a Zambezi sunset.*

RIGHT: *The traditional African cast-iron cooking pot, a standard component of the village scene – and occasionally, a feature of tourist camp life.*

ABOVE: *Canoeing on the Zambezi. The river's surface is deceptively placid; beneath are strong-flowing currents. Downstream from Kariba the flow remains fairly constant: the waters are held back and regulated by the dam, and there isn't a great deal of seasonal variation. This canoe is of the conventional kind; more unusual, and more practical, is what is known as the 'Zambezi stern-wheeler' – three boats joined together and bridged by a high deck.*

TOP: *Young mopane shoots bring the escarpment countryside to life during the first rains of summer.*

ABOVE: *One of Chizarira's long-legged little serval cats (Felis serval), a nocturnal hunter that preys on rodents, birds and small mammals.*

FAR RIGHT: *The rugged grandeur of the Chizarira, a 192 000-ha national park that sprawls across the Zambezi escarpment to the east of Lake Kariba's Binga area. The park serves as sanctuary for an impressive variety of game animals, including an unusually large number of black rhino; its bird species include the crowned hornbill (right), bat hawk and the elusive Taita falcon. Accommodation is offered by the attractive privately run Chizarira Lodge.*

**ABOVE:** *Kraal scene, in the communal lands south of Kariba: the round, thatched, mud-walled homes and elevated storage structures are typical of the region. Most Zimbabweans still follow a subsistence lifestyle in the rural areas, though hopes of a job, and the pull of bright city lights, are drawing many away from the land.*

ABOVE: *The bright and youthful face of Zimbabwe: village children drive the family donkey-cart along a rural road near Kariba. Fully three-quarters of the country's population is under 30 years of age, about 45 percent under 15, which, in a country whose economic growth potential is limited, is a source of serious concern.*
RIGHT: *The vegetation of the north-western region includes a large number of colourful xerophyte species – plants that are well adapted to dry conditions.*

**ABOVE:** *Outdoor classroom near Siwabuwa in the Kariba area. During the decade following independence in 1980 the number of children attending primary school rose from 820 000 to 2,3 million, or 92 percent of the total possible. In the same period, the number of secondary schools increased from 177 to 1 500.*

**LEFT:** *Pipe smoking is traditional among women of the Tonga group.*

**OPPOSITE PAGE:** *Spirit mediums, known as ngangas, are an integral part of religious belief and practice in Zimbabwe, acting as diviners, as intermediaries between ancestors and their living descendants, and as healers.*

OPPOSITE: *The skeletal remains of a once-dense forest rise up through the water along Kariba's shoreline. Until recently the world's largest man-made reservoir, the lake is 300 km long, 5 000 km² in area and is both a holidaymaker's paradise and an abundant source of protein-rich fish. Around and near its shores cluster some of Zimbabwe's most splendid parks and safari areas.*

ABOVE: *The fish eagle (Haliaeetus vocifer), a magnificent member of Kariba's resident bird community. Much of its diet comprises dead and stranded fish, but when it does hunt it stages an unforgettable spectacle, stooping dramatically from on high to check just before hitting the water (and occasionally plunging beneath the surface) to catch its prey.*

RIGHT: *A grey heron (Ardea cinerea) on its vantage point above the shallow waters of the lake's shore. The species tend to be solitary in habit.*

**LEFT:** *Sightseers take to the waters of Kariba's Tiger Bay area. The lake and its surrounds offer boating, water-skiing, scuba-diving, some of the most exhilarating freshwater sport fishing in the world (for the predatory tigerfish), magnificent game-viewing and scenic splendour.*
**BELOW:** *A school of hippo stays cool in the heat of a Kariba summer's day. The animal's appetite matches its huge (up to two-ton) bulk: a good day's feed for one adult is around 130 kg of grass.*
**OPPOSITE PAGE:** *Common waterbuck (Kobus ellipsiprymnus) on the Ume river-bank. These large, shaggy-coated antelope – the male weighs up to 270 kg – are found in herds of up to 30, invariably grazing near water, in which they take refuge if threatened.*

**RIGHT**: *A sturdy Kariba passenger and supplies ferry offloads at the fishing village of Msampa. The larger and better known car-ferry, 'Sealion', operates out of Andora harbour at Kariba and takes 22 hours to cover the length of the lake. Andora is a busy place of yachts, houseboats and fishing rigs; farther up the shore are enchanting little bays and inlets that enclose marinas and hotel resorts. Of these, the Mediterranean-style Caribbea Bay hotel complex is perhaps the most strikingly attractive.*

**BELOW**: *Canoeing at Tiger Bay – one of several water sports enjoyed by leisure-bent visitors. The lake's waters are gentle enough at most times, but sudden storms can whip up dangerously high waves.*

**BOTTOM**: *The yellow of a cassia species brightens Kariba's shoreline.*

Msampa is one of Lake Kariba's larger fishing communities, a dusty, sprawling village of thatched, mud-walled houses inhabited by people of the Tonga group. Much of their ancestral land was inundated during the birth of the lake in the 1950s, and about 50 000 people had to be resettled beyond the future water-line – a controversial move, vigorous-ly opposed by their leaders. The lake, though, has brought a fair degree of prosperity to the villagers. Their oddly shaped rigs annually net about 12 000 tons of a tiny sardine-like species called kapenta, a valuable and much-needed source of protein for humans and staple food for the predatory tigerfish (above) so favoured by sporting fishermen. The lake in fact sustains some 40 kinds of fish, among them the deep-bodied tilapia, or Kariba bream, a standard and delicious item on Zimbabwean restaurant menus.

OPPOSITE PAGE: *Fothergill, one of Lake Kariba's larger islands (it supports a permanent safari camp), was named after Rupert Fothergill, the game warden who, in the 1950s, orchestrated the rescue of thousands of game animals stranded by the rising waters of the lake. 'Operation Noah' captured world headlines.*
ABOVE: *Buffalo in the Matusadona national park, a splendid 1 400-km², game-rich area abutting on Lake Kariba. The park offers three exclusive rest-camps and the luxurious Bumi Hills safari lodge.*
RIGHT: *A fish eagle surveys its domain from it's rocky perch.*
PREVIOUS PAGES: *Reed cormorants (Phalacrocorax africanus) roost in the branches of a long-dead forest as the last of Kariba's light fades.*

LEFT: *This attractive red-winged pratincole (Glareola pratincola) is displaying in defence of its nest, a shallow scoop in the ground near water's edge (above left). The insect-eating species – the only wading bird that hunts on the wing – is generally uncommon except in Zululand and parts of Zimbabwe, where it can be seen in flocks near rivers and lakes and on the edges of wetlands.*

ABOVE: *Wary impala in the Matu-sadona national park, on the southern shore of Lake Kariba. Among the park's larger predators are lion, leopard and spotted hyaena.*

LEFT: *The timid, rarely seen side-striped jackal (Canis adustus) favours open plains country and a diet of carrion, though it also feeds on small mammals, ground-roosting birds and their eggs, on insects and, occasionally, on the wild fruits of the veld. The species is rather larger than its cousin, the black-backed jackal (C. mesomelas) - it weighs around 9 kg, as opposed to the latter's 7 kg – and is easily identified by the white stripe on its flanks and the white tip to its tail. Both species have long, pointed muzzles and erect ears, and are nocturnal.*

LEFT: *A monitor lizard, or leguaan (family Varanidae) peers out from its 'home' in a termite mound. These giant reptiles, of which there are two southern African species, grow to a length of up to 2 m. Both types use their forked tongues as sensors, much in the manner of snakes.*
BELOW: *These colourful carmine bee-eaters (Merops nubicoides) belong to a nesting colony in the Matusadona national park. Each pair will produce clutches of four to five white eggs in August and November. Though they roost in groups, carmine bee-eaters – which, despite their name, feed on a variety of insects, including grasshoppers – hunt and forage as individuals, invariably in the vicinity of streams and marshes.*
OPPOSITE: *Waterbuck at Matusadona, with their attendant cattle egrets.*

105

ABOVE: *Buffalo feed on the rich mix of aquatic and land grasses that flourish between Lake Kariba's high- and low-water marks.*

RIGHT: *A National Parks game-guard examines elephant spoor in the dusty remoteness of the Mat-sudona, a magnificently pristine wilderness that sprawls along Lake Kariba's southern shore*

OPPOSITE PAGE: *A splendid elephant bull emerges from the cooling waters of the lake. These giants of the African bush are placid creatures, usually 'tame' enough to allow one to approach within a few metres. But do so with caution, especially if there are small calves in the group. Keep movement and noise to the very minimum, and be prepared to drive off quickly if warning signs appear – if, that is, one of the adults turns full on to face you, raises its trunk and flaps its ears.*

*Sunrise on Kariba. The lake has dramatically transformed this segment of the Zambezi valley. It has always been a harsh land, hot and dry, inhospitable, but the great expanse of water now supports new and lusher ecosystems that have encouraged the growth of game and other wildlife populations. The shoreline grasses are exceptionally nutritious; the decomposed vegetation of the drowned forests and the notorious Kariba weed (Salvinia molesta) - a free-floating fern that once threatened to choke the lake – have enriched the waters, encouraging the proliferation of insects, of some 40 species of fish and of other aquatic life forms that sustain crocodile and hippo and a large number and variety of birds.*
*BELOW: Among the lake's waterbirds is the black-winged stilt (Himantopus himantopus), a wader that occasionally swims. In flight its long red legs trail well beyond the tail.*

LEFT: *A kapenta rig returns to harbour with a good night's catch. The locals have evolved a clever snaring technique: after the tiny fish have been attracted to the surface by lights, a net is positioned below them, the alarm given and the kapenta driven back down into the depths by noise and sudden darkness to be caught and hauled up in their thousands.*
BELOW: *Kariba's dam wall: a massive, 128-m-high concrete arch that spans the narrow, 600-m gorge of the Zambezi River between Zimbabwe and Zambia. The hydroelectric power station is on the northern (Zambian) bank.*

ABOVE: *The attractive Caribbea Bay small-craft marina at Kariba.*
RIGHT: *A pair of red-billed fire finches (Lagonosticta senegala; the male, with its distinctively pink face, throat and breast, is on the left), a very common species, found in Arabia and in Africa from Senegal down to South Africa's eastern Cape region. The bird, a familiar and endearingly tame visitor to suburban gardens, both nests and feeds (on a variety of seeds and insects) on the ground.*

LEFT AND ABOVE: *Downstream from Kariba, in the Zambezi floodplain of the Chikwenya region, is a forest of giant ana trees (Acacia albida), one of the largest of the acacia species. They grow to a height of around 30 m, and their thick, reddish, protein-filled pods are greatly relished by game animals – and especially by elephants, who will rise up on their hind legs to reach the loftier branches. Even more nutritious is the fruit of the area's numerous sausage trees (Kigelia africana): the tubular pod weighs up to 10 kg and its fibrous, seed-filled pulp, together with the cup-shaped flowers, provide a rich source of food for antelope and other animals. The fruit also has medicinal properties, and is a prime component of herbalists' remedies.*
ABOVE RIGHT: *Jeff Stutchbury leads a party of visitors through the dense Chikwenya grasslands.*
RIGHT BELOW: *The three-banded courser (Rhinoptilus cinctus) is a nocturnal, extremely agile bird. In Zimbabwe it is found in open woodland country, near rivers or on the alluvial floodplains.*

LEFT: *In typical posture, a bushbuck ram peers through the dry tangle of trees and undergrowth. Shy and mostly nocturnal, bushbuck are essentially browsers (though they will sometimes feed on grass) and, when alarmed, will emit a deep bark and run for the nearest cover.*
ABOVE: *A species indigenous to the Zambezi floodplain is the poison vine (Strophantus rombe), whose sap contains a highly toxic alkaloid that serves as both a curative source (of strophanthin, a heart stimulant) and as a destructive one (its seeds and other parts have been used for poison-tipped arrows).*
OPPOSITE PAGE: *Baboons on the move and, left, atop an enormous termite mound in the Chikwenya area of the floodplain. The chacma (Papio ursinus) is the only baboon species indigenous to southern Africa. Troops of some 50 to 100 strong, led by a few full-grown males, forage and hunt in both open and wooded country for wild fruits, bulbs, roots, scorpions, insects and such small vertebrates as hares, birds and even, occasionally, for young antelope. Their principal natural enemy is the leopard.*

OPPOSITE PAGE: *A herd of impala traverses the Zambezi floodplain in the Mana Pools area.*
ABOVE: *Hippo on the move. These massive semi-aquatic animals, up to two tons in mass, are usually found in schools of between five and 20, resting in or alongside water during the daylight hours, foraging close to the water's edge at nighttime. When the grazing is poor, however, they will travel up to 30 km in a single eight-hour period in search of fresh feeding grounds. They are excellent swimmers, and can also walk on the river-bed in deep water, remaining submerged for up to five minutes at a stretch. The calves, which are dropped in clearings trampled in the dense reed-beds, are able to swim within a few minutes of birth.*
RIGHT: *The excitement of game-viewing on the Zambezi River.*

The Mana Pools national park and its associated safari areas – almost 11 000 km² of low-lying country along the middle reaches of the Zambezi below Kariba – is a wild kingdom without parallel. Here, the sluggish, northward-flowing river has created rich deposits of alluvial soils, and channels and shallow pools in which the summer waters collect. The moisture and the lush vegetation – acacia, mopane and a feast of sweet grasses – attract huge numbers of animals and birds. OPPOSITE PAGE: Aerial view of the area just upstream from Mana Pools. The park offers two eight-bed lodges, a caravan-camping ground, a hutted rest-camp, and two superb camp sites. ABOVE: A pair of saddlebilled storks (Ephippiorhynchus senegalensis), a large species easily identified by its red-and-black banded bill and the yellow 'saddle' at the bill's base, seek their aquatic prey in the marshes of Mana Pools.

OPPOSITE PAGE: *The mysterious and magical Chinhoyi caves, carved from the soft limestone of the Hunyani hills a little over 100 km northeast of Harare. Centrepiece of the complex, which is a popular stop-off on the way to Kariba, is the Sleeping Pool, a 90-m-deep, motionless, irridescent body of water that has its place in legend: in the local Shona dialect it is known as the 'pool of the fallen', a reference to those victims of ancient clan warfare who were done to death and entombed in the cave vaults.*

ABOVE: *The eland (Taurotragus oryx) is the largest of southern Africa's antelopes: males reach a mass of some 700 kg and a shoulder height of 1,7 m. They are gregarious browsers, often seen in large herds in habitats ranging from open savanna to light woodland.*

ABOVE RIGHT: *Pamuzinda, an exclusive safari lodge in the Selous area – an hour's drive from Harare – offers superb game-viewing, five-star cuisine, and luxurious accommodation.*

RIGHT: *One of the Pamuzinda's black rhino. The private reserve specializes in the conservation of endangered species.*

Harare, the Zimbabwean capital, is an attractive city of modestly proportioned but elegant modern buildings, wide thoroughfares and a proliferation of flowering trees and shrubs – feathery, lilac-coloured jacaranda, African flames, crimson poincianas, poinsettias, pink, purple and white bauhinias and, everywhere, the tropical stridency of bougainvillea. The place, known as Salisbury until Zimbabwe's independence a little over a decade ago, began life in September 1890, when Cecil Rhodes's Pioneer Column chose the site for its final encampment and then disbanded to become the country's first white settler community.

**ABOVE LEFT**: Harare city is laid out according to a strict grid pattern; streets run north-south, avenues east-west. Union Avenue, shown here, bisects the central area.

**LEFT**: The shopping mall in Borrowdale, Harare's northernmost suburb. Features of the area are the spacious residential properties and a fine racecourse.

OPPOSITE PAGE, ABOVE RIGHT: *Harare flower-seller. The city's main flower-market fringes African Unity Square, an attractive public space known until recently as Cecil Square.*

RIGHT: *Harare's avenues, and especially those to the north of the central area, are beautifully embowered. This splendid canopy of jacaranda trees (family Bignoniaceae) displays its fantasia of blooms in springtime.*

BELOW LEFT: *One of the more eye-catching of the 'balancing rock' formations to be found in the countryside around Harare.*

BELOW RIGHT: *Contemporary Shona stone sculpture is a distinctive art form, internationally acclaimed since it first began to develop in earnest in the early 1960s. Today, according to the experts, at least five and perhaps as many as seven of the world's finest sculptor-carvers are Zimbabwean. This figure was photographed at Chipinge village near Harare. Fine examples may be seen in Harare's National Gallery, whose past director, Frank McEwen, helped pioneer the Shona school.*

ABOVE: *The Pentecostal religious movement is strong in Zimbabwe, and especially so in and around Harare. The various groups are distinguished by, among other things, their open-air form of worship, evangelical sermons, biblical-style costume and charismatic leadership, by their practice of adult baptism in the Holy Spirit through total immersion, and by their belief in prophecy and divine healing. About three-quarters of Zimbabwe's population is Christian or part Christian.*

LEFT: *An Edwardian building in the older part of Harare. Few relics of the early colonial past remain in the central business district.*

LEFT: *Harare's charming Presbyterian church, on Samora Machel Avenue, (formerly Jameson Avenue), is dwarfed by the tall, crescent-shaped, concrete-and-glass bulk of the exclusive five-star Monomotapa Hotel.*
BELOW LEFT: *Some 40 km to the north-east of Harare is the Ewanrigg botanical garden, a lovely 250-ha expanse of natural vegetation encompassing a cultivated area famed for its cycads and aloes. The former are regarded as 'living fossils', descendants of immensely ancient seed-bearing plants that appeared on earth 150 million years ago, reaching their ascendancy 100 million years later – that is, before the advent of flowering species. Ewanrigg also contains a wide variety of other endemic plants (many of them labelled) and an impressive array of bird species.*
BELOW: *The distinctive Aloe excelsa is indigenous to Zimbabwe.*

LEFT: *A few kilometres to the northeast of Great Zimbabwe lies Lake Mutirikwe (formerly Lake Kyle). Third largest of the country's reservoirs, Mutirikwe was created in the 1960s to supply water to the Lowveld's huge sugarcane and citrus plantations and, as a bonus, to serve as a recreational area. The dam wall is some 300 m long and 63 m high; the lake, at its optimum size, covers 90 km², and has a wonderfully varied shoreline. The islands it encloses are home to a fascinating variety of birds. On and near its shores are a well-appointed rest camp, caravan sites, boat clubs and, in the 90-km² park, a proliferation of wildlife (among the animals are white rhino, buffalo, giraffe and an especially impressive variety of antelope species). The lake itself, in years of good rains, sustains hippo, crocodile and a wealth of aquatic creatures, but a succession of savage droughts during the 1980s and early 1990s played havoc with water levels and took devastating toll of both the wildlife and the region's farmlands.*
BELOW: *Burchell's zebra in the pristine woodlands of the Mutirikwe park near the lake.*

*Great Zimbabwe, near Masvingo in the south-central part of the country, is a massive collection of high-walled granite structures that served as the headquarters of the ancient Karangan state. Its three main components – hill complex, valley complex and Great Enclosure – were built between AD 1000 and 1200, and for three centuries thereafter the Karangan kings ruled over much of today's Zimbabwe, their power and wealth derived from the cattle and crops of a fertile land, from the gold and iron of the region, and from trading relations that went far beyond the shores of southern Africa. Great Zimbabwe is now a declared World Heritage Site.*

OPPOSITE PAGE: *This conical tower – reminiscent of a giant grain basket, symbol of abundance – stands within the Great Enclosure.*

RIGHT: *Mortar was unknown in that time and place; walls and passage-ways were built of a myriad inter-locking pieces of stone.*

BELOW: *The Great Enclosure, viewed from the hilltop 'dzimba dzembabwe' – (houses of stones).*

**LEFT AND ABOVE:** *Portraits of rural Zimbabwe. The great dome-like granite formation shown here is typical of the middleveld countryside to the south of Masvingo (the name means 'rocks' in the local language). The town, the first to be established by the 1890 colonists, is a thriving centre of the agricultural, ranching and mining industries; gold, chrome, copper, asbestos, beryl, tin and lithium are all worked in the area. Tourism also plays a major role in the local economy; Lake Mutirikwe is in the area, as are the imposing, ancient structures of Great Zimbabwe.*

133

LEFT: *A selection of traditional earthernware pots and jars. Many of the more visible legacies of ancient Zimbabwean custom and usage – including costume, regalia and ornamentation – have not withstood the passage of time and the encroachment of western culture, but pottery – for which the Shona have always been famed – still flourishes in parts of the country. The pots are fashioned from clay; the decorations, many of them geometrical designs handed down through the generations, are added after firing.*

LEFT AND BELOW: *In the Wedza area some 40 km from Marondera is the Markwe cave, renowned for the San (Bushman) artwork that decorates roof and walls. The 'canvas' is dominated by the huge outline of an elephant; some of the paintings are of dead antelope: they lie in supine positions, with their heads and tails hanging loosely. The cave, set 55 m above the surrounding countryside and 8 m in depth, once served the local Shona as a refuge from marauding Ndebele groups; minor openings have been walled in with granite boulders and mud plaster.*

RIGHT: *This rather attractive plant, Tephrosia longipes, is a familiar species of the Zimbabwean veld. The country boasts a fine array of indigenous flowers, among them the lovely flame lily (Gloriosa superba), whose long, wavy-edged petals vary in colour from blood-red to pure yellow and are often patterned in shades of both. A flame lily diamond brooch was presented to Princess (now Queen) Elizabeth during the 1947 royal visit, after which it became accepted as the country's national flower.*

135

*For sheer scenic splendour few regions of Africa can compare with Zimbabwe's Eastern Highlands – the spine of mountains that straddles the country's border with Mozambique. The high ranges – Nyanga, Vumba, Chimanimani – are mantled by natural forests and dense plantations of pine and wattle; below are valleys rich in their bounty and stunning beauty. The region is a holidaymaker's paradise.*
OPPOSITE PAGE: *The Nyangombe River, downstream from the spectacular Nyangombe falls in the Nyanga Mountain national park.*
LEFT: *'World's View', in the Nyanga uplands. The vantage point, near Troutbeck Inn, is 2 160 m above sea level and the vista, on a clear day, is breathtaking.*
BELOW LEFT: *A common waterbuck, one of several antelope species resident in the Nyanga Mountain national park.*
BELOW: *The silent remains of Fort Nyangwe, one of a necklace of ancient enclosures that girds the lower slopes of Inyangani, the country's loftiest peak.*

OPPOSITE PAGE: *The Pungwe river-valley, 250 m below the magnificent Pungwe falls in the Nyanga region. From here the waters flow eastward to drop a further 800 m to the Mozambique plain and thence to the Indian Ocean north of the substantial maritime centre of Beira.*
ABOVE LEFT: *The Nyanga highlands afford splendid opportunities for the holidaymaker generally and the trout fisherman in particular.*
BELOW LEFT: *The celebrated Trout-beck Inn, just beyond the northern boundary of Nyanga Mountain national park. The hotel, long-established and with a devoted clientele, offers unpretentious luxury in the most splendid of surrounds, a golf course, and a private lake well stocked with trout.*
ABOVE: *The handsome purple-crested lourie (Tauraco porphyreolophus), a bird of the evergreen forests, is a common though somewhat elusive resident of the Eastern Highlands.*

RIGHT: *Much of the eastern region is classed as communal land, occupied by peasant farming families who follow traditional lifestyles and who, in most years, have enjoyed a fair degree of prosperity. Across the board, communal farmers have accounted for 80 percent of the increase in the national maize crop since independence in 1980; many have diversified into the more 'difficult' crops (tobacco and barley among others). Still, land hunger is one of the constants in Zimbabwe, much debated in the political arena. In 1992 the government announced plans for the compulsory purchase and redistribution of around 5 million hectares of the country's largely white-owned 'maize and tobacco belt'. The move came during the worst drought in history.*

LEFT: *Two women of the Nyanga area. The old ways die hard in much of rural Zimbabwe.*

ABOVE: *Tea plantations in the Honde Valley are an attractive, and economically important, feature of the Eastern Highlands.*

ABOVE AND FAR LEFT: *Mutare, capital of the eastern region, is a graceful town in the most spectacular of settings: mountains of breathtaking splendour surround it on all sides.*
LEFT: *Part of the lovely La Rochelle gardens near Mutare. The property, graced by fine displays of orchids, rare trees and ornamental shrubs, was bequeathed to the nation by the late Sir Stephen and Lady Courtauld.*
PREVIOUS PAGES: *The msasa-mantled foothills of the Nyanga range. These trees provide glorious shows of colour in springtime.*

**LEFT AND BELOW:** *Beneath the high Vumba range lies the Burma valley, a 12-km-long, heat-hazed, humid, immensely fertile area that yields splendid crops of tea, tobacco, seed potatoes and tropical fruits. Pictured are some of the irrigated banana plantations. Above the valley, on the slopes that reach up to a lofty ridge called Himalaya, there is a wealth of fascinating plant life that includes, among other species, yellowwood and cedar trees, proteas, everlastings and arum lilies.*
**ABOVE:** *Mother and child. Zimbabwe's population, which totalled something over 10 million in the early 1990s, is increasing at around 3,5 percent a year – one of the world's highest growth rates. Many schools have been built since independence in 1980 – an investment that should pay fine dividends.*

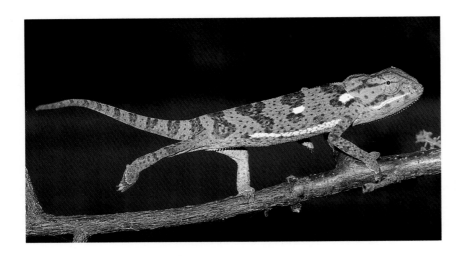

LEFT: *The common or East African chameleon (Chamaelo dilepis) is found throughout Zimbabwe. These slow-moving arboreal lizards change colour when disturbed or threatened, and to conform with their environment. They capture their insect prey by shooting out their club-tipped, sticky tongues to a remarkable distance (equal to and even more than their body length).*

RIGHT: *The reed frog (Hyperolius marmoratus), common in the eastern uplands. Breeding colonies produce a deafening night-time cacophony.*

RIGHT: *The Chimanimani range, which forms the southern segment of the eastern rampart, is a magical region of craggy krantzes, deep valleys, sparkling streams and waterfalls, of forest, grassland and heath, the whole combining to recall the distinctive character of South Africa's south-western Cape region. Almost the entire range falls within the Chimanimani national park; nearby are two much smaller but, in their way, equally special areas: the Chimanimani eland sanctuary (the eland is the only large antelope to thrive among pine plantations), and the exquisitely lovely Chirinda Forest botanical reserve.*

OPPOSITE PAGE, FAR TOP RIGHT: *The enchanting Tessa's Pools, near the Outward Bound mountain school in the northern corner of the park. The adventure courses, designed primarily for youngsters, foster initiative and resourcefulness.*

OPPOSITE PAGE, BOTTOM: *Leucospermum saxosum is one of the several protea species that bring bright flashes of colour to the upland slopes. These and a great many other plants can be seen in the Chimanimani's 150-ha Rusitu Forest botanical reserve.*

OVERLEAF: *Workers in the ploughed fields of the lovely, and hugely fertile, Burma valley.*

150

ABOVE: *The countryside in the Birchenough Bridge area is dry, rather bleak, forbiddingly hot in the summer months. From here the Save, one of the country's major watercourses, flows south to cross the Lowveld and then, after being joined by the Runde, runs eastward through Mozambique to discharge into the Indian Ocean.*

LEFT: *The delicate Rhodesian pimpernel (Tricliceras longepedunculatum) is a decorative feature of the Zimbabwean roadside. Grazing animals tend to avoid the species (it has a repellant odour), but butterflies of the Acraea genus find it tasty.*

OPPOSITE PAGE: *Travellers driving from Great Zimbabwe to the Eastern Highlands cross the Save River by way of the single-arch Birchenough, built in 1935 and ranked at the time as the world's third largest suspension bridge. Apart from the difference in size, it is an exact replica of Australia's larger Sydney harbour bridge (both were designed by the celebrated engineer Ralph Freeman).*

OPPOSITE PAGE: *Kwali camp, near the wall of the Malilangwe dam, one of two Cresta Sandstone safari lodges on the 30 000-ha Lone Star ranch adjacent to the Gonarezhou national park. The ranch is sanctuary to a huge variety of game, including elephant, black rhino, lion, leopard, buffalo and a host of antelope.*

TOP RIGHT: *The massive sandstone Chilojo cliffs in the Gonarezhou national park rise dramatically from the Runde river. These natural formations are notable both for their geological origins and for their beauty.*

RIGHT, BELOW: *Fine examples of rock art can be found among the overhangs near Kwali camp.*

BELOW: *Game-viewing in the wilds of the extensive Lone Star Ranch.*

FAR RIGHT: *One of Gonarezhou's many giraffe (giraffa camelopardalis). These are the tallest of land mammals, the bulls attaining heights of up to 5,5 m. However, despite their size, their mastery of camouflage and their lethal defensive kick, they are vulnerable to the predations of lions. The park, 5 000 km² in extent, sprawls over the low-lying, hot, flattish mopane country fringing Mozambique and close to South Africa's famed Kruger national park. Many of the larger animals move freely over the borders.*

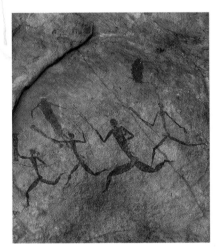

ABOVE: *A spotted genet (Genetta tigrina), one of two southern African species of the family Viverridae. These nocturnal little carnivores, long-bodied, short-legged and extremely agile, are essentially terrestial, though they are as much at home in trees as on the ground.*
RIGHT: *The Kori bustard (Otis kori), a large ground-living bird (it will fly if need be, but reluctantly), is a common resident of southern Africa's drier and more remote savannah wildernesses and a familiar sight in the Gonarezhou park.*

ABOVE LEFT: *This blue-tailed skink belongs to the Scinidae, one of the largest groups of southern African lizards. All the skinks have smooth, shiny scales but otherwise vary greatly in apperance and habit: there are tree-, rock- and ground-living species, and others that burrow.*
OPPOSITE PAGE: *Gonarezhou is famed for its baobab trees. The species, Adansonia digitata, is instantly recognizable by its strange shape and huge trunk, which can reach a girth of 28 m. Those with a diameter of 8 m and more are thought to be over 3 000 years old.*
ABOVE: *The baobab's fruit: large, with a woody shell, and much favoured by game animals. The shell houses a white pulp containing tartaric acid and potassium bitar-trate (or 'cream of tartar') which, when mixed with water, makes a refreshingly palatable drink.*
OVERLEAF: *The Nyamasakana River winds its way through the rugged landscape of southeastern Zimbabwe.*
FOLLOWING PAGE: *A herd of sable antelope. The species (Hippotragus niger) is easily identified by its large size (up to 230 kg), its magnificent scimitar horns and its conspicuous black and white facial markings.*

# INDEX